Unearthing
Family Tree Mysteries

Ruth A. Symes

PEN & SWORD
HISTORY

First published in Great Britain in 2016 by
PEN AND SWORD FAMILY HISTORY
an imprint of
Pen and Sword Books Ltd
47 Church Street
Barnsley
South Yorkshire S70 2AS

ISBN 978 1 78346 350 3

Printed and bound in England
by CPI Group (UK) Ltd, Croydon, CR0 4YY

Typeset in Times New Roman by
CHIC GRAPHICS

Pen & Sword Books Ltd incorporates the imprints of Pen & Sword
Archaeology, Atlas, Aviation, Battleground, Discovery,
Family History, History, Maritime, Military, Naval, Politics, Railways,
Select, Social History, Transport, True Crime, Claymore Press,
Frontline Books, Leo Cooper, Praetorian Press, Remember When,
Seaforth Publishing and Wharncliffe.

For a complete list of Pen and Sword titles please contact
Pen and Sword Books Limited
47 Church Street, Barnsley, South Yorkshire, S70 2AS, England
E-mail: enquiries@pen-and-sword.co.uk
Website: www.pen-and-sword.co.uk

Contents

CONTENTS

Acknowledgements

Many people have helped me in the writing of this book. Thanks first to members of my family: Michael Barlow for technical help of all kinds (particularly concerning the images) and for providing the initial idea for the book; Colin Daniels for permission to publish a page from his father (Jack Daniels') diary; Teddy Hargreaves and Elsie Ireland for memories and information on the Symes sisters; Margaret McMenemy for some of the information on George and Mary Wilkinson; the Sachak family (particularly Kurban Sachak and Ruby Karimjee) for information on their father Taibali Essaji Sachak; Amir Sachak, for providing a rare book on East African Asians in Tanganyika; Ruky Sachak for some of the old photographs of East Africa; Zara Sachak for the image of East African-Asian food; Naomi Symes for general historical assistance; Olive Symes for her memories of her Wigan roots; and Wilfred Wilkinson for his image of the Leeds-Liverpool canal.

Thanks to friends: Eric Lloyd for the images from his passport; Tim New for a variety of images including the Gladwin Family Bible; Paul Ogden for encouraging my interest in certificates and censuses years ago; Anne Sheinfield for some of the information on Jewish sayings and eating habits; and Ian and Betty Summers for the pictures of the Higham Family Bible.

I would also like to express my gratitude to various archivists, librarians and researchers up and down the country for their assistance in many aspects of this project. These include Boots Archives for the images of Boots' newsletters, Gail Collingburn from the Company Secretary's Office at WHSmith for the images of the WHSmith staff magazines; Alan Davies, archivist, Wigan Record Office for information on Wigan miners; Alison Gill, Information Officer, Greater Manchester County Record Office, for general advice on images of Manchester; Roger Hull, Researcher, Liverpool Record Office, Liverpool Libraries, for the pictures of Liverpool in the Blitz; Ron Hunt for the pictures of nineteenth-century Wigan; Roy Maber (Martock genealogist) for the images of Martock, Somerset; Diane Miller, Solicitor, for permission to publish the images of early Marks and Spencer branches; Emma Marigliano, Librarian, The

ACKNOWLEDGEMENTS

Portico Library, Manchester, for access to images of old Manchester; Kirsty Shields, archive assistant, Marks and Spencer for finding the images of the branches; Tameside Record Office for providing the obituary of Elizabeth Symes from the Stalybridge Reporter; Somerset Record Office for the images of *Kelly's Directory for Somersetshire and Devonshire*; Milton Wagy, Librarian, the Ellensburg Public Library, Washington for the images from the Roslyn Washington Image Collection; Charlotte Wand, Assistant Librarian, The Portico Library, Manchester, for providing the images of old Manchester; and the UK Passport Service.

Final and greatest thanks to my husband Zainul Sachak for his unfailing support and encouragement in all aspects of this project.

Introduction

Everyone's family history is made up of stories: some sad, some shocking, some humorous and some extraordinary. We can summon up – fairly easily (and especially so with the aid of a computer) – the essential names and dates that give our ancestors a basic identity again. But, whilst the discovery of such factual information can be thrilling, it is vital to understand that family history research can also bring far greater satisfactions. Sensing the character of a person (previously known only from a photograph) come to life as you unearth his or her past; piecing together, from mere fragments of information, the drama of a catastrophe that changed the family fortunes forever; debunking the myth that surrounds a significant family event; these are undoubtedly the real pleasures of family history.

Today a vast amount of information is available to help you to tell the stories of your ancestors' lives. You will, of course, need the official sources, – birth, marriage and death certificates and census returns – but you can also learn a great deal from many other, less likely, sources. This book aims to show you how to find this information and what to do with it in order to tell the tales that will make your past vibrant and meaningful. With its help, you will do more than add more branches to your tree diagram. Rather, you will start to tease out the many stories of your family in the past and learn to imagine them in their true place in history. Before long, the joys, tragedies and oddities of your ancestors' lives will start to unfold themselves before you in all their colour, variety and unexpectedness.

Stories from your Family Tree

The stories in this book are from my family – but they touch on themes that are common to many families in Britain. On my mother's side (from as far back as I have cared to trace) I am descended from Lancashire mill workers and miners. Their history is about the poverty and dangers of the industrial world. My father's family, on the other hand, originate from Somerset. My paternal great-grandfather moved from the West Country to Manchester (over 300 miles) in the 1880s to find work – a fact which

Family photos are most helpful where they portray several generations in one place. The Gillings family (including my father, grandfather, grandmother and great-grandfather), York, c. 1936. (Author's collection)

caused me to wonder about the way people migrated from one place to another in the nineteenth century. My husband's family, by contrast, is from outside Britain, from Tanzania and before that from India (something that has enabled me to include a chapter in this book on Empire and immigration). From all these strands I have picked twelve stories that I believe might resonate with the tales in your own family.

The Stories behind the Sayings
Each chapter of this book takes its title from a family saying or anecdote: 'He didn't come from round here', 'We come alive behind shop counters', 'Great-grandfather lived with the Red Indians'. No doubt, there will be similar cryptic remarks floating around in your family. Although

inevitably time can distort and alter them – rather in the manner of Chinese whispers – there is nearly always a glimmer of truth in sayings passed down through the generations. You may have wondered whether such remarks (and the silences that may have followed them) indicated embarrassment, distaste or reverence for the ancestors to whom they referred. This book will show you how it is likely that behind the few words, a host of half-forgotten stories lie waiting to be discovered: stories with plots, characters, settings and – should you choose to invent them – moral messages, as well.

The Shape of your Past – Plots
Whilst love plays its part, the plots of family history tend to revolve around money: the making of it and the losing of it. You may come across tales of transformations from 'rags to riches', and equally across stories that follow the opposite trajectory and describe tragic falls from splendour. You may use your family stories to measure how far you have risen from your humble origins; or to blame the noble ancestors who gambled away the family fortune and relegated their offspring to the ranks of mere shopkeepers. You may, on the other hand, decide simply that your family narrative has come full circle: 'from clogs to clogs [in] three generations' – as the saying goes.

Whatever the overall shape of your family story, you will find that there are staging posts along the way. Official and unofficial sources will help you to pinpoint the moments at which your family fortune changed direction: a period spent in prison, for example, a move abroad for work, or the death of a child. You will also unearth the less dramatic elements and episodes of your ancestors' lives – where they dwelt, if they travelled, what they did for a living, how many times they married, how many children they had, and when and how they died. This is a straightforward list in some ways, but it is one with as many variations as there are people on the planet.

Good Fellows and Scoundrels – Characters
Each significant event in your family history moves the story on and each one will have had its effect on the hero – your ancestor. Rather than staring at a static name on a family tree diagram, you will find yourself speculating on how his or her character developed as a result of his or her experiences. A villainous forebear, for example, may have turned to

religion after a spell in prison; a virtuous girl may have lost her honour; a poverty-stricken farm labourer may have inherited a fortune. As you research your stories, you will also come across a host of minor characters who may have aided your ancestor in his or her journey through life – the lodger who helped pay the rent, the employer who provided sickness leave or benefit, the charitable benefactor whose generous will kept your family out of the workhouse. Equally, you may find that your ancestor's progress was thwarted by the actions of a malevolent relative or by a disastrous chain of events initiated by someone not even known to them.

The Historical Backdrop – Settings
What our ancestors got up to was partly down to their unique personalities, but their life opportunities were also down to the setting and times in which they lived (in other words their social and historical circumstances). They may have moved from Scotland to Liverpool because work was hard to find; they may have exchanged a job in domestic service for one in the mills because wages were higher; they may have taken advantage of new, faster, methods of transport to travel abroad. These – and other historical factors too numerous to mention here – provide the background and the explanation for many aspects of the story of your ancestor and they cannot be overlooked.

The Meaning of the Past – Moral Messages
Once you have the key elements of your family story, you will find yourself speculating about what this or that event 'meant' for the history of your family. You might make up your mind, for example, that that if only your great-grandfather had stayed in Yorkshire rather than going to seek his fortune in London, he would have inherited the family mansion instead of squandering the little he had. Be aware that in adding a moral to your tale, you will, of course, be fleshing out the facts with your own interpretations and imaginings. Be careful with the conclusions you draw from your stories but enjoy them. Such speculation can be extremely satisfying and even cathartic: providing possible explanations for why you and your family are now the way you are.

INTRODUCTION

The Strange Affair of Margaret Daniels

One example from this book may suffice to give its flavour. On my family tree, the name of my great-great aunt 'Margaret Daniels' (above an all-too-short set of dates 1862–74) begged some investigation. I was intrigued to find on her death certificate that she had drowned at the age of twelve on 8 March 1874 in the Leeds-Liverpool canal. This fitted with the dark pronouncement – made to me several times by older members of my family – that the waterways in Wigan had, on occasion, 'polished off' some of my ancestors. The certificate stated that Margaret was 'carrying an umbrella' at the time of her death. When I looked in the local paper for a record of the event, the plot thickened. The report from the inquest stated that on the evening of her death, Margaret had met her brother by the canal and that later she had been seen walking down the canal bank 'behind two men'.

Such titbits from the press sent my imagination into orbit. Where was the brother at the time of Margaret's death? Who were the two men? Perhaps Margaret was murdered. Perhaps she was raped. Other newspaper reports of deaths from around the same time enabled me to

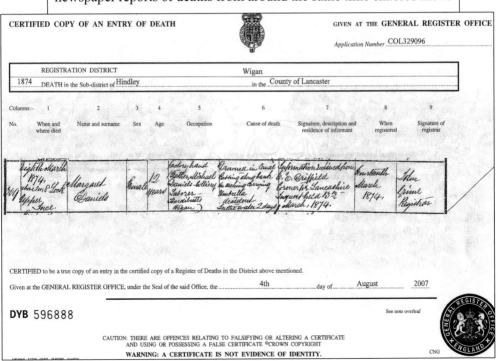

The death certificate of Margaret Daniels, 1874. (General Register Office)

NER, MARCH 13, 1874.

The enigmatic account of the death of Margaret Daniels in *The Wigan Examiner*, 1874. Transcript of Newspaper Report, 13 March 1874.

FOUND DROWNED: The body of Margaret Daniels aged 12 years, was found on Tuesday in the Leeds-Liverpool Canal, between the ninth and tenth lock, Aspull. Deceased, who was the daughter of Michael Daniels of Hardybutts, left her brother at the top lock at 7 o'clock on Sunday night, and walked down the canal bank behind two men. On Monday, her umbrella was found in the water, which led to a search being instituted, resulting in the finding of the body.

(The microfiche of *The Wigan Examiner*, 13 March 1874. With thanks to Mr P. M. Ogden)

6

understand how dangerous that canal actually was: indeed it was a locus for homicides, suicides, infanticides and abortions. Slowly but surely, I was unearthing the long lost story of a real person – a young girl who was careful enough to take an umbrella out with her when she went walking, but not careful enough to avoid drowning in a canal. I had the setting, I had the characters and I had a couple of possible reasons for her death. The result of all this is that Margaret's entry on the family tree is no longer a bald statement of the facts of her short life; it is attached to a narrative that reverberates with possibility. Briefly, she lives again.

Ancestors Within Living Memory

For many people like me researching their family tree, going back just a few generations, provides enormous – and sufficient – satisfaction. Seeking out only Victorian, Edwardian and early twentieth-century ancestors rather than those from further back gives you the chance to make direct connections between those people and your own parents, your siblings, your children and yourself. By contrast, you might find that ancestors from the eighteenth, seventeenth and sixteenth centuries, are not only more difficult to research, but also perhaps too far in the past to be of any real relevance to your life today.

The agreeable thing about our great-grandparents is that although they inhabited a somewhat different world, they are – at least a little – like us. The people in your family history who will probably most excite your curiosity are those about whom you already know a little something. They are likely to be the subject of some bizarre family anecdotes and apparently tall stories: the great-uncle who was' washed overboard ship', for example, the great-grandfather who 'chased pineapple chunks under the sideboard', the cousin who 'married two sisters (but we don't talk about him)'. In all likelihood, it is these ancestors within living memory – those not known to you directly but known to those who have known you – who will be the ones that you first want to investigate.

Despite the fact that they may have died more than a century ago, you will find that some of the essence of these near forebears remains in your family. There may, for example, be objects in your family home bought or made by relatives from the nineteenth and early twentieth centuries. You may wear your great-grandmother's wedding ring, or still make cakes

The wedding of my grandparents, William John Symes and Alice Gillings, York, 1927. I have inherited her hair and her wedding ring. (Author's collection)

baked to her recipe. If you have photographs of your great-grandparents and great aunts and uncles, you will have wondered if you look like them; if you have their letters or diaries, you will have questioned whether their reactions to life are in any way similar to yours.

Your ancestors probably live on in other ways too: in the advice, for example, that is passed down in your family to future generations, and in family sayings, turns of phrase or sense of humour. You may have inherited from your Victorian forebears a particular attitude to money, or to risk, certain habits of religious observance, eating habits or customs. The experiences of those people three or four generations back are not yet irrelevant – you will find that they have left their mark in the long, collective memory and psyche of your family.

Understanding the Story: Methods
This book recommends three main methods by which you might arrive at a better understanding of your family stories. The importance of talking to relatives; the importance of considering a wide variety of physical objects, documents and other sources (including such items as passports, recipe books, ornaments and songs); and the importance of understanding the times in which your ancestor lived. Not one of these methods takes precedence over the others – all three go hand-in-hand. You may, for example, learn something from a conversation with a relative that prompts you to look at an ornament or a certificate in a different way, alternatively, you may find a historical news item which will prompt a relative to remember more detail. And all of this information will be of greater use to you if you have an understanding of the way things worked in the past.

a) Talking to Relatives
Chatting to as many relatives as possible – and as many times as possible – when you are doing family history research really does pay off. There is always the chance that an odd detail will emerge that could lead you into new realms of investigation. To maximise the likelihood of this happening, you might try a number of strategies:

• Use prompts – items that you can hold and examine such as commemorative tankards and photographs can provide great talking-points.

• Put the questions in different ways on different occasions. For example, to ascertain when certain events happened, rather than asking the date, ask whether or not a certain family member was born at that time. Rather than asking simply about facts (which many people may be unable to recall), ask about feelings, for example, 'How do you think Uncle Charlie felt about the move/the marriage/the birth of so many children?' Such open questions allow people to talk freely and this is when unexpected information may slip out.
• Make sure you double-check when accounts given by relations seem to be contradicting each other. Incorrect memories can be as interesting as correct ones. There may be a significant reason for them.
• Always ask – on the off chance – whether there is anything in print (or written down) about the story you are discussing. Relatives often have newspaper clippings, diaries, old school magazines, autograph books and many other items that they assume will not be of any interest to anyone tucked away. You can nearly always learn something from these.

b) Documents, Objects and Other Sources

Use your conversations with your relations in tandem with as many sources as you can lay your hands on. You may not have the time, energy or resources to do too much hands-on research in record offices, but you may actually already have a wealth of untapped material in your home. Re-examine the contents of your attic and your garage; take another look at the ornaments on your mantelpiece, at the engraved plate on the clock in the hall; and rummage through the documents in old piano stools and suitcases – you might find a company newsletter, an old menu or a swimming certificate, which just might tell you something you didn't know about your ancestor.

And don't stop there: flick through the books on your shelves for bookplates and meaningful scribbles; question your relatives about the existence of a family Bible; attempt the recipes in the family recipe book; write down the words of the songs with which your mother sang you to sleep; and try to remember the exact expressions your grandfather used when the weather was cold or when he was feeling ill. All of these sources may point you towards more facts about your ancestors (the bookplate may send you off in search of your great-grandfather's school, for example) but – more importantly – they will give you a feel for the colour and shape of their lives. In simple, everyday objects, papers and information passed down by word of mouth, you will find clues to your ancestors' tastes, their wealth, their education, their geographic mobility, their religious beliefs and many other things.

You will, of course, find many other unusual sources to aid your family history research on the internet. Gems such as obsolete maps of towns, A-Zs of old occupations, telephone directories for defunct London boroughs, and lists of the symptoms of tuberculosis and cholera (diseases which might have claimed your ancestors' lives) all appear online. There is no excuse for using the computer simply as a means of adding to the facts, facts, facts of your family tree. You should use it – as you should use all your sources – to help you tell an interesting story.

c) Researching the Times
To flesh out your ancestor's tale, you will need to find out more about its setting and its circumstances – for instance, you may find information on the industries and companies active in the town in which he lived; the way people travelled during the years he was alive; how, as a representative of a particular trade, he is likely to have dressed; the likelihood of him dying from certain diseases, and a whole host of other things. Remember, your ancestor was not only an individual but also a member of a community: be it a Lancashire mining town, a Scottish fishing village, an old Catholic family or a Jewish immigrant district in a big city. Finding out more about the history of the relevant community will help you find out more about the story of your ancestor. You may not find out *exactly* what happened to him or her, but you will gain an understanding of what was likely and what was impossible. This is where family history overlaps with social history. And, you can bet that whatever historical scenario you are interested in – whether it is prostitution in nineteenth-century London or grouse shooting on the Yorkshire moors – there will be a book or a website somewhere that will be able to help you.

How to Use this Book
Unearthing Family Tree Mysteries has been written to help you in your quest to really understand your ancestors and to tell their stories. You may read this book in two different ways. Enjoy it as a series of stories which might well touch on the historical themes that have characterised your own family history (industrialisation, domestic service, war, etc); and

learn from it how to use key sources (such as newspapers, passenger lists and passports).

The 'Resources to Take You Further' sections at the end of each chapter suggest a variety of books that may help you if your family stories cover similar areas to mine. They also include a list of relevant websites and useful addresses. A complete bibliography also appears at the end of the book.

Stories and Histories

First and foremost, this book is a set of stories about a bunch of characters from the past. They include: the aspiring farm labourer who left Somerset for a new life in the industrial North West; the Lancashire mill girl who lost six children probably as a result of a sexually-transmitted disease; the young girl who may have been pushed to her death in the Leeds-Liverpool canal; the boy who watched the Blitz from above a shoe shop in Liverpool; and the Indian lad who crossed the ocean to make his fortune. There are plenty of other, more minor, characters too who may be characteristic of the communities in which your ancestor once lived: the faceless boarders and lodgers of the Manchester slums, for example, and Lancashire washerwomen and miners, domestic servants, grocers and shop girls.

The stories cover a number of themes that have dominated British history over the past 150 years. Chapter 1 looks at **economic migration** between different parts of Britain in the late nineteenth century. Chapter 2 considers **poverty, disease and child mortality** in Lancashire between 1860 and 1885. Chapter 3 examines the phenomenon of **boarding and lodging** in working-class communities in the same period.

The **dangers of life in industrial towns** (particularly in mines and canals) is examined in Chapter 4 whilst Chapter 5 looks at a first-hand account of **the Blitz** on Liverpool during the Second World War. Chapter 6 is about **rituals surrounding death** in the middle of the twentieth century.

Chapter 7 looks at the way in which some **large employers** catered for the welfare of their employees in the last decades of the nineteenth and first decades of the twentieth century. Chapters 8 and 9 take on a more international dimension, examining respectively **emigration** to America in the late nineteenth and early twentieth centuries and **immigration** to Britain from other parts of the **British Empire** (particularly India and East Africa) in the mid-twentieth century.

INTRODUCTION

The hidden **domestic lives** of women are examined in Chapter 10, whilst Chapter 11 considers **cultural tastes and family relationships** from the evidence of a bookcase. Chapter 12 shows how what we eat can reflect the **geographical origins, culture, religion and wealth** of our ancestors.

Key Sources
The second half of each chapter is about sources. You will learn how to access them and what information you are likely to obtain from them. In a section entitled 'Think Laterally', you will be given some tips on how to think about these sources so that you get the most out of them.

Chapters 1 to 3 focus on some traditional family history sources. Chapter 1 takes **trade directories** and asks what they can tell you about the places from which your ancestor came. **Birth, marriage and death certificates** are examined in Chapter 2 and I look at how the information in these can be strung together to form meaningful narratives about the lives of individuals. Chapter 3 takes that vital genealogical tool – **the census** – but looks at a somewhat neglected aspect of it – the records of those people who were registered as boarders and lodgers.

Chapters 4 to 6 look at some slightly more unusual sources which you may find lying around the house or amongst old family papers. Chapter 4 shows how **newspaper** accounts can add detail to stories that otherwise can only partially be glimpsed in certificates. Chapter 5 examines the most personal source – a **diary** – and asks what its contents can tell you both about the life of an ancestor and the times in which he or she lived. Chapter 6 takes a number of bits of paper relating to death such as **obituaries, mourning cards and burial plot certificates** and asks what the details of a funeral can tell us about a person's life.

Chapters 7 to 9 examine sources that can tell you more about your ancestors' lives outside the immediate vicinity of their home. Chapter 7 uses a **company newsletter** as a starting point for examining the lives of ancestors who worked for large firms. **Passenger lists** (which might help you to find out more about ancestors who emigrated to America or went there to work) are the subject of Chapter 8. Chapter 9 uses **passports** to look at relatives who may have come to Britain from other parts of the British Empire.

Chapters 10 to 12 look at some unofficial and more unusual sources that you may never previously have considered as evidence. **Oral history** (particularly songs and sayings) are covered in Chapter 10. Chapter 11 looks at the **books (including the Bible)** that your family might have inherited and what these can tell you about the education, aspirations and wealth of your ancestors. Chapter 12 looks at the way **family recipes and eating habits** can indicate various aspects of our origins.

Finally, as you research your own family stories, remember that if they concern ancestors from just a few generations ago, they are about people who are relatively near to you in thought, experience and emotion. Consider this: I have been kissed by a man who was kissed by a man born a hundred and fifty years ago. The kiss nearest in time was from my grandfather William John Symes (1894–1968) who kissed me as a baby in 1966. He, in turn, was, no doubt, kissed by his father, William Symes, who was born as long ago as 1855.

You can probably say something similar about yourself.

Resources to Take You Further
Books

Barratt, Nick, *Who Do You Think You Are? Encyclopedia of Genealogy: The Definitive Reference Guide to Tracing Your Family Tree*, Harper, 2008.

Catlett, Estelle, *Track Down Your Ancestors: Draw Up Your Family Tree*, Elliot Right Way Books, 2003.

Chater, Kathy, *How to Trace Your Family Tree in England, Ireland, Scotland and Wales*, Hermes House/Anness Publishing, 2006.

Cole, Jean A., Armstrong, Michael, and Titford, John, *Tracing Your Family Tree: The Comprehensive Guide to Tracing Your Family History (Genealogy)*, Countryside Books 2003.

Galford, Ellen and Ancestry.com, *The Genealogy Handbook: The Complete Guide to Tracing Your Family Tree*, Reader's Digest Association, 2005.

Gill, Anton, and Barratt, Nick, *Who Do You Think You Are? Trace Your Family History Back to the Tudors*, HarperCollins Entertainment, 2006.

Herber, Mark, *Ancestral Trails: The Complete Guide to British Genealogy and Family History*, 2nd edition, Sutton Publishing, 1997.

Hoskins, W. G., *Local History in England*, 3rd edition, Longman, 1984.

Osborn, Helen, *Genealogy: Essential Research Methods*, Robert Hale Ltd, 2012.

INTRODUCTION

Rogers, Colin, *The Family Tree Detective: Tracing Your Ancestors in England and Wales*, Manchester UP, 1997.

Rogers C., and Smith, J. H., *Local Family History in England. 1538-1914*, M.U.P., 1991.

Waddell, Dan, *Who Do You Think You Are? The Genealogy Handbook*, BBC Books, 2014.

Websites

www.ancestry.co.uk Large collection of resources including censuses, birth, marriage and death indexes, shipping lists, military records etc.

www.cornucopia.org.uk Database of more than 6,000 collections in UK museums, archives, galleries and libraries.

www.discovery.nationalsrchives.gov.uk Description of millions of records held by The National Archives and more than 2,500 other archives.

www.familysearch.com Family history information compiled by the Church of Jesus Christ of the Latter-day Saints (including baptism and burial records).

www.ffhs.org.uk Federation of Family History Societies.

www.findmypast.co.uk Research your UK ancestry.

www.genuki.org.uk Large collection of genealogical information pages for the UK and Ireland.

http://www.local-history.co.uk/ Links to many local history sites.

www.nationalarchives.gov.uk The National Archives.

www.sog.org.uk Society of Genealogists Family History Library and Education Centre.

www.thegenealogist.co.uk British Genealogy Research website.

CHAPTER 1

'He Didn't Come from Round Here'

Focus on History: Migration within Britain
Key Source: Commercial and Trade Directories

Finding out where your ancestors lived is crucial to understanding how they lived and what their sense of the world was like. Though many of us like to imagine that our forebears lived in the same place since time immemorial, a little research often disproves this fact. You may be surprised to find that ancestors just a few generations back came from a totally different part of the country. In particular, many people migrated from one part of Britain to another during the Industrial Revolution of the late eighteenth and early nineteenth centuries. You may have an inkling that your great-grandfather came from Cardiff, or Cornwall or Newcastle, but how do you find out more about his city, his town or even his parish of origin? It will be important to you to understand why he moved and to speculate on how he might have felt about the huge changes of lifestyle that this must have entailed. One place to start is by examining the commercial or trade directory for the town or village in which your ancestor once lived.

The Story
The photograph taken in a studio on Peter Street, Manchester in 1894 shows what appears to be a typical urban family of the late-Victorian period. My paternal great-grandfather, William Symes, is the very picture of Mancunian civic respectability as he poses in his dark suit and white shirt, with his wife Elizabeth (née Terrell) and their five daughters, Phyliss, Annie, Jenny, Lilly and Emmie. With this image in my mind, I was surprised one day when one of my elderly aunts remarked darkly of William that he 'didn't come from round here'. On further questioning, she told me what she knew – that William had moved to Manchester from

Great-grandfather William Symes and his family, Manchester 1894. William's family knew nothing about the secrets of his earlier life in Somerset. From left to right, Phyllis, Annie, William, Jenny, Elizabeth, Lilly and Emmie Symes. My grandfather John William (the last child) was born after this photograph was taken. (Author's collection)

the town of Martock in Somerset in about 1883 when he was 28 years old. There was something about the way in which she revealed this information that suggested that I should ask no more questions. Things, it seemed, had happened in Martock that were best forgotten!

I looked back into the eyes of the man on the photograph and saw someone who was not a natural city-dweller at all, but a country boy who had exchanged sunshine and apple trees for the drizzle and soot of a monstrous Northern city. Why had he done this? Was there some motive beyond the search for work? Many British people did migrate from one town to another during the nineteenth century but, generally speaking, professional people and those with special skills moved more often and further than those of the labouring classes, like William. I could see that his migration from Martock to Manchester – a distance of nearly 350 kilometres – was no small undertaking. He must have known when he left Somerset that he would not be able to go back easily. In fact – as far as my aunt knew – he never went back. What, if anything then, had he left behind?

The Man from Martock

To understand William and his migration better, I needed to find out more about the place he had come from – the village of Ash, near Martock. But Somerset is a long way from Manchester (where I currently live) and I was hesitant about making a long journey south without any real idea of what I was looking for. What I needed was something that would tell me

Man of mystery: William Symes (1855–1907). Photographed c. 1894 in Manchester. (Author's collection)

about the essence of the place at the exact time that William lived there (between his birth in 1855 and his leave-taking in about 1883). To my delight, a simple internet keyword search under 'Martock' revealed that the Victorian trade directory, *Kelly's*, for the town of Martock in the year 1875 had been transcribed and was available online. The relevant volume of a trade directory can quickly provide you with a fascinating snapshot of life in a particular town in a specific year in the past.

Kelly's Directory of Somersetshire and Devonshire, 1875. Trade directories provide a wealth of useful local information. (By permission of Somerset Archive and Record Service)

Transcript from *Kelly's Directory for Somersetshire and Devonshire* (1875). Pages relating to the town of Martock.

MARTOCK is a village or town, with a station on the Yeovil branch of the Bristol and Exeter railway, and gives the name to the hundred in which it is, situated 130 miles from London, 5 south-west from Ilchester, in the Mid division of the county, Yeovil union and county court district, Ilchester rural deanery, archdeaconry of Wells, diocese of Bath and Wells, and province of Canterbury. The church of All Saints is a very fine building: it has handsome carved oak nave roof, and five-light Early English eastern window: the clerestory is an excellent specimen of the Perpendicular style: the organ, which has been restored, is very good: the seats are of oak, and there are several mural tablets. The parish registers date from the year 1553. The living is a vicarage, yearly value £272, with residence and 60 acres of glebe land, in the gift of the Treasurer of Wells Cathedral, and held by the Rev. Edwin Arthur Salmon, M.A., of Wadham College, Oxford, prebendary of Buckland-Dinham, in Wells Cathedral. The old Grammar school, which stood near the church, has been pulled down: it was founded in 1661 by William Strode, of Barrington, who charged his estates with a yearly payment of £12 for its support; subsequently the manor of Martock was released from this annual payment, the lord of the manor charging certain parishes with quit rents to the amount of £15 5s. 7d.; these quit rents, however, were not regularly paid, and ultimately the trustees placed the matter in the hands of the Charity Commissioners, who sold the old buildings in 1871; the whole of the trust then amounted to £347, and quit rents £10 15s. 2d., payable annually, and is now used to promote generally the education of boys and girls in the hundred of Martock, no fresh school having been built. There are National schools for boys and girls, and a Sunday school is held in the school-room. There are chapels for Independents and Baptists. Goodden's charity, of £26 yearly value, is distributed in bread to the second poor of the parish every Sunday, and Leach's, of £9 yearly, is for clothing. There is an old cross in the market place, near the spot where formerly stood an ancient oak tree, from which this village is said to derive its name Martock (Market Oak). A fair is held the third week in August, yearly, for cattle, and a market the last

Monday in every month. The manufacture of gloves is somewhat extensively carried on here. J. Goodden, esq., is lord of the manor and principal landowner. The soil is clayey, and the subsoil is clay. The crops are chiefly wheat and beans. Flax is also cultivated in many parts. The area is 7,302 acres; rateable value, £18,700; the population in 1871 was 3,091.

ASH, LONG LOAD, MILTON, STAPLETON, WITCOME, COATE, HURST, and BOWER HENTON are tithings in this parish. ASH, MILTON, and WITCOMBE from the ecclesiastical parish of Ash, which see. LONG LOAD is also a separate ecclesiastical parish.

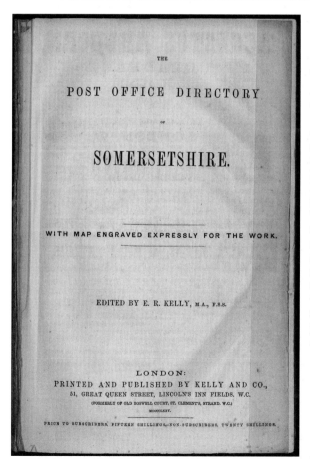

The pages on Martock from *Kelly's Directory of Somersetshire and Devonshire*, 1875 including a general description of the town, its services, a list of private residents, and mention of Samuel Sly, the carrier of Martock who perhaps facilitated William's escape. The directory also makes mention of Elizabeth Symes (probably William's grandmother) who runs a farm in the tithing of Coat and of dairyman Emmanuel Worner, who was William's uncle and who brought him up. (By permission of Somerset Archive and Record Service)

The place where the boy William Symes grew up was very different from the city in which he later came to live. *Kelly's* described the topography of the area around Martock, as a land of 'clayey' soil between the Parret and Yeo rivers where wheat, beans and flax grew. The vistas of William's youth then were the very opposite of the narrow streets of terraced houses in Ancoats and Beswick (the poor districts of Manchester) to which he migrated.

Although William himself was too poor to be mentioned by name in *Kelly's Directory*, I was delighted to find that a member of the family – probably his grandmother, Elizabeth Symes – was listed. Trade directories do not, as a matter of course, record female names, but, as this lady was a widow and running a farm, she was entitled to an entry. Soon I found the names of neighbouring farmers in the same tithing (Coat): the Bartletts, the Gilletts and the Rendalls. On the whole, this was a rural area and I could say with reasonable certainty that the companions of William's early life would have been ploughboys, sheep boys, farmers' carters, dairymen and shepherds.

But what of Martock itself? In *Kelly's*, some of the local architecture is described. The old church of All Saints with its fine carved oak nave roof and oak seats, the market place with its old cross, the town's couple of schools and chapels. Compared to this small-town scene, how startling my great-grandfather must have found Manchester with its large-scale amenities, its education, water, gas, parks, police force, fire brigade, roads and graveyards all run from the central administrative building of the massive and newly-constructed town hall. Compared with the semi-rural streets of Martock, the lines of buildings in Manchester (iron foundries, boiler making plants, engineering factories, dye houses, bleach yards, banks, insurance houses and packaging warehouses) must have seemed endless.

Kelly's Directory for Martock excited my imagination by providing many other points of contrast with Manchester. The local population of Martock and the surrounding area in 1871, for instance, was just 3,091. How different from the huge and growing population of Manchester (estimated at 355,000 as early as 1861). And it was obvious from the list of names that the population of Martock was pretty homogenous – just about everybody living there was probably of English origin. In Manchester, on the other hand, William would have been an immigrant among many other immigrants, joining people on the move from

The quiet and ancient centre of Martock with the Treasurer's House and parish church. How different from Manchester's bustling Albert Square! (Roy Maber)

Germany, Eastern Europe, Ireland, and Italy as well as from many other parts of Britain. Like them, he would probably, at least in part, have renounced the ways of his homeland, worn different clothes to cope with the wetter climate, and modified his dialect to make himself understood.

According to *Kelly's*, the biggest social gathering of William's life in Martock would have been the market, held on the last Monday of every month. Everyone in the local community – blacksmiths, carpenters, basket makers, beer retailers, farmers, butter and cheese factors, coopers, dairymen and glovers – would have attended this event. Did William, I wondered, remember this rural market as he wandered years later past the museums, art galleries, libraries, theatres and parks that provided the huge population of Manchester with its entertainment? Did he contrast the delights of the yearly cattle fair in Martock (held during the third week of August every year), with the big events occurring in Manchester such as the grand opening of the great Manchester Ship Canal in 1894?

City hubbub: The Art Gallery and the Athenaeum, Manchester, as William would have known them in 1896. (From *Manchester Old and New* by William Arthur Shaw with illustrations after original drawings by H. E. Tidmarsh, Vol III. Cassell and Co., 1896, between pp. 40 and 41)

The opening of the Manchester Ship Canal, 1894 – an event which William is likely to have attended as an interested member of the public. (From *Manchester Old and New* by William Arthur Shaw with illustrations after original drawings by H. E. Tidmarsh, Vol III. Cassell and Co., 1896, p. 88)

An online map of nineteenth-century Somerset (at www.visionof britain.org.uk) enabled me to see the one thing that linked the rural South West with the industrial North – namely the railway. The Yeovil branch of the Bristol and Exeter railway must have run through the fields where the young William played and worked. It was, of course, the railway that allowed William to leave the town of his birth. *Kelly's* gives details of the weekly carriage service from Martock to Yeovil (a large and complex railway junction) by horse-drawn omnibus that picked up passengers from outside the White Horse pub. Did William send his belongings separately to the station by way of Martock's carrier, Samuel Sly, who, according to the *Directory*, conveyed goods every Tuesday and Thursday morning? And when William eventually became a Manchester man and found employment as a carter transporting boxes from Victoria Station to the various outlying suburbs, did he perhaps remember Samuel Sly, the carrier of Martock? The directory had fired my imagination. I felt that I really understood something of William's two worlds and the huge differences between them.

Street Scene

As I scrolled through the transcription of *Kelly's Directory* online, I almost felt that I was wandering past the clockmakers, blacksmiths, carpenters and stonemasons of William's youth. I could even, if I wished, envisage the variety of shops in a single street; Frederick Alexander, (miller), Samuel Culliford (butcher), Samule Lye (baker and beer retailer) and Taylor Matthias Ring and Co. (wine and spirit merchants) all operated, for example, from East Street.

Manchester Man of Secrets

Undoubtedly, the move to Manchester had many advantages for William, but I was still left wondering why he had moved so far from home. Was there something, perhaps – as my aunt had intimated – that he wished to leave behind in Martock? Inspired by the *Directory*, I set about the task of finding William in the censuses of 1861, 1871 and 1881. To my immense surprise, I discovered that in the 1881 census when he was 26, William's marital status is described as 'W', meaning widower.

William married Elizabeth Terrell – the lady in the photograph that opens this chapter – in Manchester in 1884. But she was evidently not his first wife. The five daughters in the photograph were not William's only children either. I searched the marriage indexes for William's first marriage and finally discovered that he had married a Martock girl, Emma Talbot, in 1878. Further research revealed that they had had a child, Ida Symes (who incidentally was conceived out of wedlock). Emma and Ida died within a few months of each other in 1878 and are buried in a Martock graveyard! It was strange to think that had they lived, William would probably never have migrated to Manchester.

I will never know whether it was to escape the sadness of the deaths of Emma and Ida that William moved so far from Martock. But I have speculated that it made him feel better to put a large part of the country between himself and that mound of earth in the local churchyard. *Kelly's Directory* itself, of course, did not reveal William's secrets, but finding out about where he lived as a young man, and understanding the huge transition he must have made physically and mentally between the small rural town and the large urban city, helped me to understand how he had managed to keep his secrets so safe. William's move North gave him a kind of anonymity. He was able to start again, and to become a true 'self-made' man in the nineteenth-century sense of the expression.

William's children from his second marriage – including my grandfather who was his youngest child and only son – would live their lives as urban people with no knowledge of that earlier marriage and their half-sibling. Though only a train journey away, Martock remained, to them, an almost mythical place of cider and sunshine, alluded to occasionally by the grown-ups, but somewhere that was firmly in the past.

Key Source: Commercial and Trade Directories

Commercial and trade directories are a good source of information about cities, towns and parishes in the nineteenth century. Most directories were produced from the 1850s onwards. The best-known directories are *Kelly's*, *Pigot's* and *Slater's*, but many local firms also published directories of their own counties or areas.

Information in directories was collected in different ways. Sometimes, agents toured the neighbourhood and visited every house: sometimes postmen circulated questionnaires. Occasionally information was cribbed from earlier editions or even from other commercial directories. Beware, therefore, of the potential for errors.

Where can I find commercial and trade directories?
Directories relating to the towns from which your ancestors originated may be found:

- at www.historicaldirectories.org. This is a digital library of local and trade directories for England and Wales from 1750 to 1919. It is produced and owned by Leicester University. You may search for the directory you require by location, by decade or by keywords
- online and free, if they have been transcribed by other family historians interested in the same area. Simply google the name of the town in which you are interested plus 'historical directories' and see what comes up
- as hard copies in larger reference libraries, local history libraries and record offices
- as hard copies in the Guildhall Library, London
- as published facsimile editions (check any online bookselling site eg. www.amazon.co.uk). In addition, some of the current popular family history magazines have produced CD Roms that have included trade directories for certain towns. You would need to search the back issues catalogues of these magazines to see if the town you are interested in is represented.

Information in trade and commercial directories is often listed in several different ways. Your ancestors may appear in an alphabetical list of householders, or under the trade they practised, the street they lived in, or under an official position that they held.

What can I find out from commercial and trade directories?
Directories often include:

- a description of the local area, its rivers and mountains, its natural resources and agricultural produce
- a short history of the area
- population statistics
- statements regarding administrative areas
- mention of Poor Law Unions
- charitable institutions (such as almshouses)
- lists of gentry, clergy, farmers, tradesmen and craftsmen
- names and addresses of private residents

- names of local Justices of the Peace
- adverts for businesses
- names of churches and chapels
- schools
- pubs
- dates of local markets and fairs
- stagecoach and railway connections
- times of local carriers' arrivals and departures
- times of local mail deliveries
- large folding maps of the area.

Think laterally

Unless your ancestors were reasonably well off, their individual names will not appear in commercial and trade directories. You will not, for instance, find the names of ordinary labourers and the poor, nor will you find the names of people living in a house other than the householder (even if the occupants are of the middle or upper class). If your ancestor ran a farm or business, his name will be recorded, but the names of his wife and children will not.

Commercial and trade directories are most useful for building up a picture of the place in which your ancestors lived. If they moved from one part of the country to another, compare trade directories from both places at the time of the migration. Ask yourself what your ancestor might have gained by the move and what he or she might have lost? What are the significant differences between the two places and how might your ancestor have felt about them?

From trade directories, you can make an educated guess about all sorts of aspects of your ancestors' lives. You can imagine, for example, where they worshipped and where they might be buried. You can guess at the shops in which they bought their food and clothes, and the pubs in which they drank.

Directories can chart the changing fortunes of your family. If you look at several editions for the same town or area over a number of years, you may notice that your ancestor moved addresses within the area as his family grew or shrank and as his business changed hands.

Resources to Take You Further

Books

Maber, Roy, *Martock Memories: A Hundred Years of Village Life*,
    Norman Maber and Associates, 1975.

Maber, Roy, *More Martock Memories: The Story of a Somerset Village*,
    Matthew Maber, 1993.

Maxted, Ian, *British National Directories 1781-1819: an Index to
    Places in the British Isles Included in Trade Directories with General
    Provincial Coverage*, Exeter Working Papers in British Book Trade
    History, 1989.

Melling, Dhyll, *Historic Trade Directories in Guildhall Library*,
    Guildhall Library Publications, 2005.

Mills, Dennis R., *Rural Community History from Trade Directories*,
    Aldenham, Local Population Studies, 2001.

Norton, J. E., *Guide to the National and Provincial Directories of
    England and Wales (excluding London) published before 1856*, Royal
    Historical Society, 1950.

Shaw, G., and Tipper, A., *British Directories: A Bibliography and
    Guide to Directories Published in England and Wales (1880-1950);
    & Scotland (1773-1950)*, 2nd edition, Leicester UP, 1997.

Shaw, William Arthur, *Manchester Old and New with Illustrations after
    Original Drawings by H. E. Tidmarsh*, Vols 1–3. Cassell and Co., 1896.

Websites

www.british-history.ac.uk. Digital library of key printed primary and
    secondary sources for the history of Britain and Ireland (mainly 1300
    to 1800).

www.cityoflondon.gov.uk/things-to-do/guildhall-
    library/Pages/default.aspx London Guildhall Library which includes a
    large collection of trade directories.

www.curiousfox.org.uk. A village by village contact site for anyone researching
    family history, genealogy and local history in the UK and Ireland.

www.gazetteer.co.uk Lists 50,000 places in England and Wales and gives
    historic county, national grid reference and administrative county.

www.historicaldirectories.org. a collection of digitised trade directories,
    part of the University of Leicester's Special Collections Online,
    covering England and Wales from the 1760s to the 1910s.

www.historypin.com The History Pin website which includes

interactive maps to which people can 'pin' photos or videos of places (past or present).

www.local-history.co.uk Advice and help for the local historian including details of local history societies nationwide.

http://www.martockonline.co.uk/ Information on the town of Martock with a section on its history.

www.nearby.org.uk Resource centre for information on any location around Britain organised by postcodes.

www1.somerset.gov.uk/archives Somerset Record Office.

www.npemap.org.uk New Popular Editions Maps showing what Britain looked like at different times going back to the 1920s.

www.oldmaps.co.uk Late nineteenth-century Ordnance Survey maps of the areas in which you are interested – to buy.

www.one-place-studies.org/ Society of One-Place-Studies.

www.pastmap.com Interactive mapping tool which offers information on listed buildings, scheduled monuments, architectural, archaeological, industrial and maritime sites in any given area.

www.victoriacountyhistory.ac.uk An encyclopaedic record of England's places and people from earliest times to the present day.

www.visionofbritain.org.uk Describes areas of Britain between 1801 and 2001, including maps, statistical trends and histories.

Addresses
Guildhall Library
Aldermanbury
London
EX2P 7HH

Martock Library
North Street
Martock
Somerset
TA12 6DL

Somerset Heritage Centre
Brunel Way
Langford Mead
Norton Fizwarren
Taunton
TA2 6SF

CHAPTER 2

'Great-Great Granny Was a Rum 'Un'

Focus on History: Poverty and Disease
Key Source: Birth, Marriage and Death Certificates

The most important pieces of information that you will need as you research your family tree are birth, marriage and death certificates. Once you have gathered a number of certificates about the life of a particular person, arrange them on a table in chronological order. It helps too, if you – separately – draw up a timeline of events. Think about the time between a marriage and a birth, a birth and a death, a birth and another birth, and you will soon have an indication of the various chapters of your ancestor's

Lydia on the back of her grandson's motorbike, c. 1927. (Author's collection)

life. And then look at the certificates in more detail: focus on the ages of the key participants; look closely at the addresses and occupations given; consider who registered the events. From these details you may be able to speculate further on the exact circumstances of births, marriages and deaths. Soon, you will begin better to understand the joys and the tragedies that gave your ancestor's life its distinctive pattern. The facts you uncover may be shocking and even unsavoury, so stay open-minded and be prepared for surprises.

The Story

My great-great-grandmother, Lydia Fletcher (later Lydia Cooke, and later still Lydia Hilton), a mill worker from Wigan in Lancashire, was quite a character by all accounts. When I was a child, elderly relations told me how she would froth up her nightly pint of ale by dipping a red-hot poker into it. I found a photograph taken in the 1920s, which provided me with the startling evidence that when she was in her 80s, she liked to ride on the back of her grandson's motorbike! But alongside the fun, there was tragedy in Lydia's life. My grandmother, her granddaughter, once told me in hushed tones that Lydia had had a lot of children who had died in infancy.

This tale upset me enormously as a child. When I was older, I decided to find out whether there was any truth in it. Lydia had left precious little evidence of her life; she was a very poor woman who could neither read nor write. Her tragic story is mapped out not in any diary or autobiography but only in the birth and death certificates of her many children. Over many months, I trawled the birth and death indexes for Wigan and discovered that Lydia had registered the birth of at least eleven children (six daughters and five sons). I discovered also that my grandmother had been right in her recollection that few of these children had survived – at least six by my reckoning had died in childhood. When the 1911 census became available to view, I was shocked to discover that Lydia's answer to the so-called 'Fertility Question' (which appears on that census alone) stated that she had actually given birth to fourteen children of whom only four lived to adulthood. Why I have been unable to find certificates relating to the missing three children remains a mystery, but it is possible that they were stillbirths (which did not necessitate a birth or death certificate until a change in the law in 1927). Armed with a sheaf of birth and death certificates relating to Lydia's children from the General Register Office, however, I became aware that this was not a

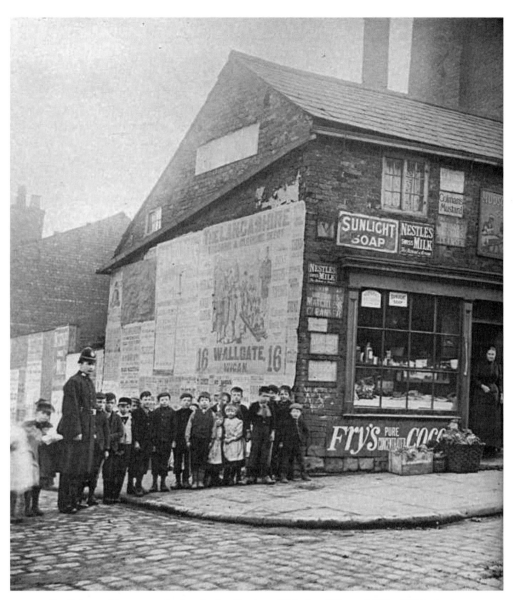

Lydia's world: a grocer's shop in the district of Scholes, Wigan, 1890s. (With thanks to Ron Hunt)

straightforward case of the high infant mortality that often afflicted poor families at the time. In fact, a rather more desperate and perhaps shameful situation lay beneath.

A Most Unsavoury Secret
From the evidence of the causes of death given on all those death certificates, it looked as though Lydia and her family must have had a terrible secret. They were probably sufferers of the dreadful sexually-transmitted disease – syphilis. Dealing with such discoveries in your family tree can be difficult. Some researchers would have left the matter there, but, having spent so much time unearthing Lydia's secret, I felt I couldn't abandon her. I wanted to know more and set about doing some research into syphilis using books and internet sites. Through this, I came to understand far more than I might otherwise have done both about the conditions in which Lydia must have lived and the troubles that she had to deal with.

Syphilis in Britain

By the mid-nineteenth century, the British government, doctors and social campaigners were vigorously debating the matter of sexually-transmitted diseases and it was the fear of syphilis, in particular, which led to the controversial passing of the Contagious Diseases Acts in the early 1860s. These Acts sanctioned the arrest of prostitutes in the seaports and their on-the-spot examination for syphilitic symptoms. With the health of the Royal Navy at stake, syphilis had become an urgent national concern.

My great-great-grandmother, Lydia did not live in a seaport, nor was she, I am reasonably sure, a prostitute. She was born in 1845 into a poor mining family in Wigan and started work as a weaver in a cotton mill. After the birth and death of her first illegitimate child, Alice, she was married twice, first to a collier, James Cooke, and then, following his death in a pit accident in 1884, to a neighbour, James Hilton. Across her two marriages, if we are to believe the evidence of the 1911 census (and why wouldn't we?) she conceived and gave birth to fourteen children.

Lydia's Children

Name	Birth	Death	Age at death	Cause of death
1. Alice	31 Dec 1864	26 Feb 1866	1	Teething/ Pneumonia
2. William	9 Dec 1867	20 May 1870	2	Croup
3. Sarah Ann	4 Jul 1870	28 Jan 1871	6 mths	Marasmus (progressive wasting away of the body)
4. Elizabeth	26 Nov 1871	28 Feb 1872	3 mths	Syphilis
5. Thomas	9 Feb 1873	28 Jan 1881	7	Convulsions/ imbecile from birth
6. Enoch James	13 Sep 1875			
7. John	26 Oct 1877			
8. Mary	22 Oct 1880			
9. William	26 Dec 1881			
10. Lydia	7 Apr 1885			
11. Sarah	5 May 1887	16 Feb 1888	9 mths	Convulsions
12, 13, 14. Three others				Possible stillbirths

Child mortality was high among the working classes of nineteenth-century Wigan. But the fact that at least half a dozen of Lydia's children died in infancy struck me as more than usually unlucky. According to their death certificates, they died from a variety of illnesses including pneumonia and croup (see table above). The family's living conditions would have been cramped, and money would have been tight; Lydia's home was just the sort of environment in which killer diseases thrived. But I started to suspect that the family had a more insidious health problem when I came across the death certificate of the fourth child, Elizabeth, born in 1871. The word '*syphilitica*' jumped off the paper and begged further investigation.

After some searching of medical websites (including http://www.cdc.

Application Number COL297007

| REGISTRATION DISTRICT | Wigan |

1872 DEATH in the Sub-district of Aspull in the County of Lancaster

Columns:-	1	2	3	4	5	6	7	8	9
No.	When and where died	Name and surname	Sex	Age	Occupation	Cause of death	Signature, description and residence of informant	When registered	Signature of registrar
115	Twentysixth February 1872 Mews of springs Aspull	Elizabeth Cook	Female	3 months	Daughter of James Cook Coal miner	Syphilitica Certified	+ The mark of James Cook Present at the death New Springs Aspull	Twenty eighth February 1872	William Clark Registrar

CERTIFIED to be a true copy of an entry in the certified copy of a Register of Deaths in the District above mentioned.

Given at the GENERAL REGISTER OFFICE, under the Seal of the said Office, the 18th day of July 2007

DYB 600077

See note overleaf

MAC

The death certificate of Lydia's daughter Elizabeth in 1872 clearly states that the cause of death is syphilis. (The General Register Office)

gov/std/syphilis/STDFact-Syphilis.htm), I realised that my great-great grandmother would have been nursing a very sick child indeed. Elizabeth would probably have been suffering from anaemia and fever. Her skin would have been yellow and covered in sores and rashes; she may have had a swollen liver and spleen, and any number of physical deformities. One description of a syphilitic baby from 1918 gives a vivid portrait of a child with the condition:

> Born at seven months of an equally syphilitic father and mother, it was a sickly creature of minuscule dimensions, a dirty yellow in colour, and so lifeless and emaciated that it hardly seemed worth taking care of it. This miserable creature was wrapped in warm wadding and placed in the best possible conditions to prevent it from getting chilled. It could hardly swallow a few drops of sugared milk or water.

(Pr Roux, *La Syphilis* (Paris, 1918) Cited in Claude Quetel, *History of Syphilis*, Polity Press, 1990, p. 166)

The Scourge of Whole Communities

But this is a story about far more than the suffering of just one child. If Elizabeth died of syphilis, I realised, then it followed that her mother, Lydia, must also have had the disease. I wondered where she might have caught it. Syphilitics can suffer for years and, in some cases, decades. Had James Cooke, Lydia's first husband, been a carrier, or did her affliction predate her marriage? Lydia's first job was in a cotton mill – a working environment in which men and women worked side by side at hard, sweaty, physical tasks, and where sexual behaviour was notoriously lax. Lydia had definitely been sexually active at this time because she had become pregnant at nineteen, two years before she married.

If Lydia caught the disease from a fellow mill worker then it is possible that it claimed the life of her first child, Alice. It had always seemed odd to me that one of the causes of Alice's death was given as 'teething'. As I read more about the symptoms of syphilis, I learnt that it can mimic the symptoms of other diseases (to the extent that it has sometimes been called 'the Great Imitator'). Moreover, I learnt that syphilitic children

The death certificate of Alice Fletcher (Lydia's first – and illegitimate – child), 1866. (The General Register Office)

often suffer problems with their teeth. Characteristically, the upper incisors are pegged and screwdriver-shaped ('Hutchinson's teeth'). I was aware that my suspicions in the case of Alice were perhaps a little far-fetched, but I still wondered whether some of Lydia's other children, whilst appearing to die from other causes, in fact, like Elizabeth, had lost their lives to 'the great scourge'.

Take Sarah Ann, Lydia's third child, for example. She is recorded as having died in 1871 from 'marasmus' – a wasting of the flesh. But, as I learnt from an internet site, (www.homepages.primex.co.uk/~lesleyah /grtscrge.htm) babies afflicted with syphilis 'looked like little old men, ill-developed, miserable, puny and wizened'. Surely the symptoms of the two diseases are too similar for me to discount syphilis as a possible cause of Sarah-Ann's death?

Then there is Lydia's fifth child, Thomas, who died at the age of seven in 1881 from 'convulsions' and is described on his death certificate as having been 'an imbecile from birth'. Children with syphilis (if they survive beyond babyhood) may have cranio-facial abnormalities, defects

The death certificate of Lydia's son, Thomas Cooke [*sic*] (described as an 'imbecile from birth'), 1881. (The General Register Office)

of the soft palate, and may suffer retardation in development generally. I believe now that Thomas was almost certainly suffering from 'neurosyphilis' – a condition that causes fits and seizures similar to epilepsy.

As well as suffering the grief of losing several children, Lydia may well have been suffering physically herself. The signs that someone has syphilis are usually out of sight in the first stage of the disease; in the second stage, they are more obvious; a skin rash on one or more areas of the body and rough red or reddish brown spots on the palms of the hands and the bottoms of the feet. Sufferers can also experience fever, swollen lymph glands, a sore throat, patchy hair loss, headaches, weight loss, muscle aches and fatigue.

Syphilophobia

'The pox', as it was vulgarly known, was unsightly and socially unacceptable and it was strongly associated with prostitution. Popular belief had it that the disease was somehow generated within the sexual organs of 'loose' women and created by their promiscuity (the role of men in the equation was often conveniently overlooked). Was Lydia vilified in her community as sexually loose, I wonder? As baby after baby died, the local neighbourhood may well have suspected Lydia's plight. And such was the general lack of knowledge about how the disease was transmitted – it was thought that it could be passed by ordinary touching or by eating food prepared by the sufferer – that she may well have suffered the characteristic hostility or 'syphilophobia' that has dogged sufferers through the ages.

As far as treatment was concerned, Lydia probably suffered in silence. Many medical institutions refused to admit patients suffering from syphilis and the twentieth-century developments of salvarsan and, much later, of penicillin were still a long way in the future. The only treatment that Lydia might have received would have been the application of mercury (rubbed on the skin or taken orally). It is unlikely, however, that she sought treatment; more likely, I feel, that the symptoms of the disease went into abeyance.

This brings me to another issue that has always puzzled me about the mortality of Lydia's children. It surprises me that after losing five children, she went on to have five healthy ones in a row, Enoch James, John, Mary (from whom I am descended), William and Lydia. Again, the

39

answer may be there in the medical literature: syphilitics, it appears, characteristically go through a phase in which the disease is latent and, during this time, female sufferers are unlikely to pass it on to any children to whom they may give birth.

After Lydia married her second husband, James Hilton, she gave birth to at least one more child, daughter, Sarah in 1887. With what horror must she have witnessed this little girl's demise and death at 9 months from the same 'convulsions' that had claimed at least two of her earlier children. At some point another three child were born and died, or possibly entered the world as stillbirths. These calamities suggest that Lydia's infection had possibly reasserted itself. Alternatively, her new husband may have been another carrier of syphilis. At 36 and never previously married, he might well have frequented the town's prostitutes earlier in his life.

The death certificate of Lydia's daughter Sarah Hilton, 1888. (The General Register Office)

40

Syphilis – A Political Disease

Syphilis was big news in late nineteenth-century Britain. Many middle-class reformers, including the redoubtable Josephine Butler, challenged the Contagious Diseases Acts because they believed that the rights of women were being violated by the authorities which were forcing medical examinations upon them without their consent. Butler's challenge to the Acts, in fact, helped to spur on the emergent Women's Movement. It is likely, however, that back in Wigan, Lydia Fletcher, who was illiterate and therefore couldn't read a newspaper, knew nothing about the important political implications of the disease that had so shaped the history of her family.

Josephine Butler (1828–1906), a Victorian social reformer who was particularly concerned with the welfare of prostitutes (depicted here in her mid-twenties). (Image believed to be in the public domain. Original held by Liverpool University)

I wondered how Lydia's own story ended. The third and final stage of syphilis is often dramatic and cruel. Sufferers incur damage to internal organs including the brain, nerves, eyes, heart, blood vessels, liver, bones and joints. I was thankful to find out that after all the miseries of her early life, Lydia managed to escape all of these horrors. She lived, in fact, until the ripe old age of 87 and continued to enjoy her frothy pint right up to the end. After all she had been through, her death certificate (in 1933) actually records nothing worse than bronchitis!

Lydia in a traditional Lancashire shawl in about 1927 when she would have been 82. (Author's collection)

41

Key Sources: Birth, Marriage and Death Certificates
Births, marriages and deaths in Britain have been formally recorded since 1 July 1837 in a process known as Civil Registration. This supplemented the traditional method of recording baptisms, marriages and burials in local parish registers held by churches. Civil Registration did not become compulsory until 1875. Registry offices across the nation sent local information to the General Register Office. This then compiled indexes of the returns for the whole country.

Birth, marriage and death certificates are the essential building-blocks of family history. Recovering them takes time and patience. Once you have them, make sure you scrutinise them very carefully – they may yield a great deal more than the obvious facts.

How can I get hold of birth, marriage and death certificates?
You will need to have the name of the person that you are looking for and some idea of when they were born, married or died. The process of searching for a certificate is then in two stages. First you must search the Birth, Marriage and Death (BMD) indexes in the period in which you are interested. Indexes are available for the four quarters of each year: the March quarter (Jan-Feb-Mar); the June quarter (Apr-May-Jun); the September quarter (Jul-Aug-Sept); and the December quarter (Oct-Nov-Dec).

The BMD indexes can be viewed:

• on microfiche in many local public libraries and county record offices
• online at a variety of internet sites including www.freebmd.org.uk, www.findmypast.co.uk, www.ancestry.co.uk and www.thegenealogist.co.uk.

Once you have located what you believe to be the correct entry for the person in your family, you need to note down the following details about their birth, marriage or death.

• the year (e.g. 1872)
• the quarter (e.g. Jan-Feb-March)
• the district name (e.g. Wigan)
• the General Register Office (GRO) reference number (which consists of a volume number and a page number e.g. 8c, 11) .

You will need all these details in order to complete the second part of the process – sending off for the actual birth, marriage or death certificates themselves. You can only be sure that the person you have seen in the index is your ancestor by sending off for the certificate.

You can order and pay for the certificate:

• online at gov.uk/gro/content/certificates
• by post or phone from the General Register Office, Southport (address below)
• in the register office that is local to where the events happened.

What can I learn about my ancestors from certificates?
Certificates are rich sources of information.
    Birth certificates usually include:

• place of birth (registration district, subdistrict, county and exact address)
• name of the child
• sex of the child
• date of birth
• first name and surname of the father
• first name and maiden name of the mother
• rank or profession of the father
• the signature, description and residence of the person who informed the registrar of the birth
• when the birth was registered
• the signature of the registrar.

    Marriage certificates usually include:

• first names and surnames of both spouses
• ages of both spouses
• condition of both spouses (i.e. whether they were widowed or single)
• occupation of the groom
• occupation of the bride (if she worked – and, even then, not always recorded)
• name and occupation of the bride's father
• where the bride and groom were each living at the time of their marriage
• names of the bride's and groom's fathers
• occupations of the bride's and groom's fathers
• where the marriage took place (church, parish, county)
• when the marriage took place.
• signatures of the bride and groom (This will tell you whether or not they were literate. If they were not, they will merely have put a cross.)
• signatures of two witnesses.

43

Death certificates usually include:

- name of the deceased person
- date of death
- where the death took place (registration district, sub-district, county and exact address)
- sex of the deceased person
- age of the deceased person
- occupation (for women this was often given as 'wife of . . .')
- cause of death
- signature, description and residence of the person who informed the register office of the death.

Think laterally

Many births will have been out of wedlock or certainly within the first nine months of marriage. If child mortality was high in the area, bear in mind that there may be several children with the same name born in quick succession in a family.

Marriage certificates should be checked carefully to see whether either party had been married before. If so, the bride or groom will be described as widowed. Divorce was very uncommon before the last quarter of the twentieth century. The addresses of married person, their occupations and the occupations of their fathers may give you some idea about where the bride and groom met. Large discrepancies in the ages of married persons also allows for some speculation about the nature of their relationship.

On death certificates, the supposedly inconsequential detail can speak volumes. Who reported the death and were they present at the death? Ask yourself whether the person died in his own home and if not, why not? If someone died from an unusual disease such as 'typhoid', check the local newspapers from the period or history books to see whether there had been an outbreak of such a disease in the area.

Resources to Take You Further
Books
Brockington, Colin Fraser, *A Short History of Public Health*, Churchill, 1956.
Davis, Gayle, *'The Cruel Madness of Love': Sex, Syphilis and Psychiatry in Scotland, 1880-1930*, Rodopi, 2008.
McHugh, Paul, *Prostitution and Victorian Social Reform*, Croom Helm, 1980.

McLaughlin, E, *Illegitimacy*, 5th edition, Federation of Family History Societies, 1992.

Porter, Roy (ed.), *The Illustrated Cambridge History of Medicine*, Cambridge UP, 2001.

Porter, Roy, and Hall, Lesley, *The Facts of Life: The Creation of Sexual Knowledge in Britain 1650-1950*, Yale UP, 1995.

Quetel, Claude, *History of Syphilis*, Polity Press, 1992.

Ward, Margaret, *The Female Line: Researching Your Female Ancestors*, Countryside Books, 2003.

Websites

www.cdc.gov/std/syphilis/STDFact-Syphilis.htm Facts about syphilis.

www.gro.gov.uk The General Register Office from which can be obtained birth, marriage and death certificates for England and Wales.

www.gro.scotland.gov.uk General Register Office for Scotland.

www.groni.gov.uk General Register Office for Northern Ireland.

www.homepages.primex.co.uk/~lesleyah/grtscrge.htm Article by Lesley Hall, 'The Great Scourge: Syphilis as a medical problem and a moral metaphor, 1880-1916'.

www.sedgleymanor.com/diseases/diseases_front_page.html Lists diseases and medical terms in a way that is helpful to genealogists.

http://library.wellcome.ac.uk/ Library on the History of Medicine.

http://www.wiganworld.co.uk/ Wigan site for Wiganers.

http://www.wlct.org/Culture/Heritage/historyshop.htm The History Shop, Wigan – a collection of archive material on this Lancashire town.

Addresses

General Register Office
Certificates Services Section
PO Box 2, Southport PR8 2JD

The History Shop
Wigan Heritage Service
Library Street
Wigan WN1 1NU

Wellcome Library (for the History of Medicine)
Part of Wellcome Collection
183 Euston Road, London NW1 2BE

CHAPTER 3

'So Poor, They Took in Lodgers'

Focus on History: Working-class Living Conditions
Key Source: The Census

The census is a snapshot of life in the family home every ten years since 1841. It can be invaluable in helping you to understand the composition of your family (their names, relationships, occupations and ages), and the make-up of the neighbourhood in which they lived. You should bear in mind, however, that the censuses record only the people who were actually in the house on census night. Family members who were living or staying in other parts of the country will not appear at their home addresses, although their whereabouts may be ascertained relatively easily these days with the aid of the online censuses. Conversely, you may be puzzled by the names and details of people who were living or staying at your family address who were not members of your immediate family. Spend a little time considering the profile of your household each decade: the number, sexes, ages and occupations (and potential income) of all the people living under one roof. Be prepared also to enter a slightly different world where ideas about such matters as 'private space' were by no means the same as our own.

The Story
As I scanned the 1891 census for the municipal ward of New Cross, Manchester, I was in for a surprise. The household of my great-grandfather, William Symes, revealed an unexpected extra member – 22-year-old Thomas Metcalf. Puzzled, I quickly ran my eye down the column entitled 'Relation to Head of Family' and the mystery was solved: Thomas was no long-lost son or cousin of the family, but that most lowly of residents – the lodger. I was immediately taken back to something that an elderly uncle had once said to me of this part of the family. 'They

were', he had said, 'so poor they took in lodgers.' This was all before the First World War and before the time when 'P.G'.s or 'paying guests' became more acceptable. My great uncle made his revelation in a tone of voice that would have been little different if he had been suggesting that my great-grandparents had been living with pigs!

Phyllis, Jenny and Emmie Symes, c. 1891. They were so young, they would probably have been bundled into the same room as their parents, thus freeing up space for the lodgers. (Author's collection)

Finding Thomas set me thinking about that small two-up, two-down terraced house at 29 Llanfair Street. It must have been quite crowded, I imagine, housing as it did not only Thomas but also my great-grandparents William and Elizabeth Symes and their three small daughters. According to the census, Thomas had been born in Farndon, Cheshire. Whatever had originally brought him the 60 or so miles to the big city, he was now, according to the census, working in the same occupation as my great-grandfather – as a carter on the railway. Perhaps, I speculated, that he had got chatting to my great-grandfather one day at work and that is how he learned that the Symes family had a room to rent!

The handwritten description of the census enumeration district in which the Symes family lived (Ancoats 52) describes an area along the River Medlock to Palmerston Street Bridge. (www.ancestry.co.uk)

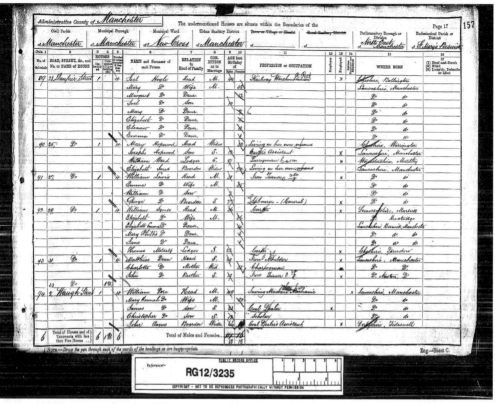

1891 census showing Thomas Metcalf, a carter, lodging with the Symes family. (www.ancestry.co.uk)

The type of back-to-back houses that the Symes family lived in. These are in nearby Salford. (From *Manchester Old and New* by William Arthur Shaw, with illustrations after original drawings by H. E. Tidmarsh, Vol III. Cassell and Co., 1896, p. 107)

Finding a Bed

Most lodgings in the nineteenth century would have been found by word of mouth. In addition, early trade organisations sometimes provided their members with lists of potential lodging houses in areas to which they intended to move. Alternatively, people might have secured lodgings by scouring the streets for advertisement cards placed in windows by prospective landlords. From the 1870s onwards, Common Lodging Houses were required by Act of Parliament to display a notice stating their status in some conspicuous place. Also from this period, names of lodging housekeepers had to be registered by urban and district councils.

When I followed the family up ten years later in the 1901 census, I noticed that, unsurprisingly, lodger Thomas had moved on, but the Symes family (now living in the ward of Bradford, Manchester) had a new paying guest, 55-year-old Hannah Perkinson – 'a weaver in a cotton factory'. Unlike Thomas, Hannah is described as a 'boarder' – a term that implies that she ate her meals with the family. The Symeses by now had a fourth daughter (a fifth had died as a baby) and a son (my grandfather). Mealtimes must have been very busy.

Thomas Metcalf and Hannah Perkinson were just two of hundreds of thousands of people who lodged or boarded in the nineteenth and early twentieth centuries. I looked on the censuses at the families who were the neighbours of the Symeses and noticed that they were from roughly the same economic group: railway warehousemen, ironturners, ironmoulders and sewing-machine mechanics – many of them had also taken lodgers in. It struck me that – whatever my uncle thought – the Symeses wouldn't have been embarrassed by their lodgers: such arrangements were evidently very much a necessary part of life in this community.

Equally, in the nineteenth century, lodging was a normal part of the life cycle for many young working-class people, and of people of all classes who increasingly had more reasons – work, education, leisure – to be away from home. Lodgers were to be found all over the British Isles in both urban and rural communities and 'lodgings' could be anything from the dreaded workhouse, to pubs, schools, dressmaking establishments, and (as the appetite for holidays increased) to boarding houses in seaside resorts. From the middle of the nineteenth century

1901 census showing Hannah Perkinson, a cotton weaver, boarding with the Symes family. (www.ancestry.co.uk)

onwards, establishments of a certain size housing several lodgers were designated as 'Common Lodging Houses' and had to follow rules and regulations laid down in the Common Lodging Houses Acts of 1851 and 1853 and other related legislation.

In cities like Manchester – where there was a severe shortage of municipal housing – it was more usual to hold a house as a tenant rather than as an owner. The setting of rents was largely unregulated and, faced with high payments, tenants like the Symes family were probably forced into subletting to avoid eviction. I was interested to find out from the history books that lodgings were invariably situated in fairly poor areas, but not, actually, in the *very* poorest areas since here severe overcrowding meant that subletting to strangers was well-nigh impossible. Census enumerators faced a dilemma when recording lodgers in their returns.

Many houses were rented in the nineteenth century and it could be argued that all the people living in a house and paying rent – such as my great-grandparents themselves – should have been designated as 'lodgers'. As it was, in this case, the enumerators chose what seemed to them the sensible option – to record Thomas and Hannah as a 'lodger' and a 'boarder' respectively and to treat my great-grandparents – who were the 'masters of the door' – as the householders.

Problems of Terminology

From the 1831 census onwards, the terms 'lodgers and boarders' were used to define guests who (unlike 'visitors') paid rent to the householder. Whereas 'boarders' shared the kitchen and dinner table with the householder, lodgers were expected to live and eat separately. Census enumerators may not always have paid heed to this distinction, however. Is it true, I wonder, that my great-grandparents' 'boarder', Hannah Perkinson, ate with the family, whilst their 'lodger', Thomas Metcalf did not? I doubt it. The chances are that the census enumerators just picked whichever term came to mind.

The Lodgers

The vast majority of nineteenth-century lodgers were young men who had moved to the industrial centres from rural areas, or indeed from other urban areas, to take up seasonal work. They included railway workers, navvies and builders who were taking part in the great processes of Victorian city construction. Lodgers also increasingly came from the aspiring lower-middle and professional classes and included shop assistants, clerks, accountants and trainee clerics. In addition, a fair number of females in trades such as dressmaking also lodged. One of the main and most obvious reasons for lodging in the late nineteenth-century was the fact that, in the absence of other forms of transport such as trams, buses and bicycles, people had to walk to work. Both Thomas Metcalfe and Hannah Perkinson would have been able to do this from their home at the Symes's. They may have lodged on a weekly basis returning to their own family homes at the weekends, or may have lodged seasonally, moving on when their contracts finished.

Whilst many lodgers in large cities were migrants from other parts of Britain, a very large number of others were immigrants seeking to establish themselves in a new country. In the 1840s, after the famine,

The Irwell at Ordsall: the environment in which the Symes family lived was heavily industrial. (From *Manchester Old and New* by William Arthur Shaw, with illustrations after original drawings by H. E. Tidmarsh, Vol II. Cassell and Co., 1896, p. 16)

many seeking bed and board were of Irish origin. In the 1860s and later, in the 1880s, thousands of Jews from Eastern Europe came to Britain, first to escape economic privation and later to escape persecution. They came, in the main, to the Northern cities of Leeds, Manchester and Liverpool, and often lodged with those members of their own families who had come before and were now better established.

Bed and Board

In return for their rent, Thomas Metcalfe and Hannah Perkinson may have rented their room 'all found' – that is, furnished by my great-grandparents. More likely, they would have been provided with an unfurnished room and would have had to provide their own effects.

The Symeses would have supplied their lodger and boarder with **'attendance, light and firing'** and I could half imagine those little girls running up and down the stairs with the necessaries.

- **'Attendance'** covered a range of services from cleaning the lodger's room to carrying water, emptying slops such as waste waters and chamber-pots, making fires, running errands and cleaning boots.
- **'Light'** meant that candles would be supplied.
- **'Firing'** suggested that coal would be provided.

Lodgers might have cooked their own meals on their own fires, or have bought their own food and paid a small sum for it to be cooked by the landlady. Male and female lodgers would have received different sorts of treatment. My great-grandmother may have done Thomas Metcalfe's washing for example, whereas Hannah Perkinson might have been expected to do her own.

I was still keen to understand my uncle's abhorrence of the practice of taking in lodgers. Certainly, there was a somewhat negative attitude by members of the middle classes towards lodgers in the nineteenth century. This was partly due to a new sense of social uncertainty. Lodgers were expected to pay for their accommodation in cash (rather than with

William Symes worked as a carter or 'townsman' at Manchester's Victoria Station. (From *Manchester Old and New* by William Arthur Shaw with illustrations after original drawings by H. E. Tidmarsh, Vol II. Cassell and Co., 1896, p. 53)

Milldom, Ancoats: one of William's lodgers worked in the mills, possibly in nearby Ancoats. (From *Manchester Old and New* by William Arthur Shaw, with illustrations after original drawings by H. E. Tidmarsh, Vol II. Cassell and Co. 1896, p. 3)

their skills as they had done under earlier apprenticeship arrangements), and landlords were no longer their masters. In novels and the press, lodging houses were popularly assumed to be dirty, and their communal facilities to foster immorality. Young male lodgers were perceived as a threat poised to defile female members of the household on the backstairs! And female lodgers too came in for censure, the assumption being that their morals were even 'looser' than those of domestic servants.

A number of laws were passed in the 1850s to try to ameliorate the conditions in some of the larger so-called Common Lodging Houses. In 1851 and 1853, the Common Lodging Houses Acts allowed specially appointed agents of the Metropolitan Police (and later the police in the provinces) the right to enter and search lodging houses at any time of the day or night to check on the numbers of people sleeping there, the mixing of the sexes in the sleeping arrangements, and the sanitary arrangements. Later acts went still further in tackling the perceived filth and immorality of some of the larger lodging houses. My great-grandparents' small-scale lodging arrangements, however, would not have been affected by these Acts.

I have concluded, however, that for all the inconveniences experienced by both lodgers and landlords, lodging was an activity that might have enriched the lives of my great-grandparents and their children. The money brought in by those who stayed with them would have helped them survive financially, but more than this, having a lodger would have brought them into contact with people from other places and other walks of life. It would have given them a window out of their back-to-back terrace onto the world.

Key Source: The Census
Censuses show us our ancestors in household groups. This allows us to imagine many aspects of their lives from their physical living arrangements and their economic situation, to how they might have run the household (for example, by identifying those who might have looked after the children whilst the others worked). Bear in mind that the censuses currently available for the general public to look at were taken on the nights of 6 June 1841; 30 March 1851; 7 April 1861; 2 April 1871; 3 April 1881; 5 April 1891; 31 March 1901; and 2 April 1911. Knowing the exact date can sometimes be helpful. If family members whom you expected to be there are not present, consider the fact that they might have joined the army, been in prison, been serving on a ship, or been working elsewhere.

How do I get to look at a census?
These days, by far the easiest way to find your family on the census is to go online. The internet has several sites where censuses from all over the country have been put together in one place (see 'Resources to Take you Further: Websites'). Many sites now have access to all the censuses from 1841 to 1911. Simply type in your ancestor's name and (preferably) some details of his/her address. Knowing your ancestor's approximate date of birth can also help. You may be able to locate some census details about your ancestors for free, but to see the whole entry, you will often have to pay.

Alternatively, if you are looking for censuses that cover your local area, copies of these will be held on microfilm in your local County Record Office or in your local library. The local census may well have been indexed either by street or by family name. Make sure you ask the Librarian if such an index exists, as this can save you hours of work.

What information about my ancestor can I obtain from a census?
The first page of a census for a particular area can be interesting in that it will give you (as a written description) the route taken by the census enumerator on the night the census was taken. The names of the principal roads in the area will be given and noteworthy buildings will be mentioned. These details can be your first indication of the environment – the bridges, cottages and warehouses, for example – in which your ancestors once lived.

The 1841 census for England and Wales gives:

• the address at which the household lived (this can sometimes be very vague)
• the name of every member of a household
• the age of every member of a household (rounded down to the nearest five years)
• the sex of every member of a household
• the profession, trade, or employment of each member of the household or whether they were of independent means
• whether each member of the household was born in the county in which the census was conducted.
• whether each member of the household was born in Scotland, Ireland or Foreign Parts.

The 1851 to 1881 censuses for England and Wales give:

• the address at which the household lived
• the name and surname of every member of a household
• the age of every member of a household
• the sex of every member of a household
• identification of the head of household
• the relation of others to the head of the family
• the condition of each member of the household as to marriage
• the rank, profession or occupation of each member of the household

- where each member of the household was born
- whether a member of the household was blind, or deaf and dumb (1851 and 1861), blind, deaf and dumb, imbecile or idiot, or lunatic (1871 and 1881).

The 1891 census for England and Wales gives:

- the address at which the household lived
- the name and surname of every member of a household
- the age of every member of a household
- the sex of every member of a household
- identification of the head of household
- the relation of others to the head of the family
- the condition as to marriage
- the profession or occupation of each member of the household
- where each member of the household was born
- the number of rooms occupied by the family (if fewer than five)
- whether each member of the household was an employer, an employee, or neither employer or employee
- whether each member of the household was deaf and dumb, blind, a lunatic, an imbecile or idiot.

The 1901 census for England and Wales gives:

- the address at which the household lived
- the name and surname of every member of a household
- the age of every member of a household
- the sex of every member of a household
- identification of the head of household
- the relation of others to the head of the family
- the condition of each member of the household as to marriage
- the profession or occupation of each member of the household
- where each member of the household was born
- the number of rooms occupied by the family (if fewer than five)
- whether each member of the household was an employer, worker, on their 'own account', or working at home
- whether each member of the household was deaf and dumb, blind, a lunatic, imbecile or feeble-minded.

'SO POOR, THEY TOOK IN LODGERS'

The 1911 census for England and Wales gives:

- the address at which the household lived
- the name and surname of every member of the household
- the age last birthday of every member of the household
- the sex of every member of the household
- particulars as to marriage of each member of the household:
  - marital status;
    - for each married women entered
    - total number children born alive
    - number of children still living
    - number of children who have died
- personal occupation of each member of the household:
  - precise branch of the Profession, Trade, Manufacture etc
  - particular kind of work done, article made, material worked on or dealt in
  - industry or service with which the worker is connected
  - whether employer, worker or working on own account
  - whether working at home
- birthplace of each member of the household
- nationality of every person in the household born in a Foreign Country:
  - in the UK, the name of the County Town or Parish
  - part of the British Empire, Dependency, Colony, Province, State
  - other Foreign Country
  - at sea
  - whether Resident or Visitor in the UK.
- infirmity of each member of the household (if any);
  - totally deaf or deaf and dumb
  - totally blind
  - lunatic
  - imbecile or feeble-minded
  - the age at which the person became afflicted
- number of rooms in the home (including the kitchen but not including the scullery, landing, lobby, closet, or bathroom, and also not including warehouse, office or shop).

Think laterally
Compare entries for your family in one census with entries in the census

of a decade later. Did any children die between the two dates? How has the household changed shape over the course of the decade? Would more or less money be coming into the house in the later period? Would there be more or less room?

Use censuses in conjunction with maps of the area in the period in question (see useful websites below). Think about where your ancestors lived in relation to farmland, rivers, main roads, train stations, churches and chapels.

Don't forget to scroll up and down the census around the entry for your ancestors. Take a look at the households of their neighbours. What kind of jobs did these people do? Did they have roughly the same income as your family, do you think? Were the families roughly the same shape as yours or was your family unusual in some way?

Resources to Take You Further
Books
Davidoff, Leonore, 'The Separation of Home and Work? Landladies and Lodgers in Nineteenth- and Twentieth-Century England', in Burman, Sandra, *Fit Work for Women*, Croom Helm, 1979.
Gibson, J. S. W., *Local Census Listings*, Federation of Family History Societies, 1992.
Higgs, E., *A Clearer Sense of the Census: The Victorian Censuses and Historical Research*, HMSO, 1996.
Higgs. E., *Making Sense of the Census; The Manuscript Returns for England and Wales, 1801-1901*, HMSO, 1989.
Hindle, B. P., *Maps for Local History*, Batsford, 1988.
Lumas, S., *Making Use of the Census*, 4th edition, PRO, 2002.
Walton, John, *The Blackpool Landlady*, Manchester UP, 1978.

Websites
www.1911census.co.uk The 1911 census only can be accessed here for a fee.
www.ancestry.co.uk All the available censuses can be accessed here for a fee.
www.familyhistoryonline.net The Federation of Family History Societies provides information on local censuses.
www.findmypast.co.uk All the available censuses can be accessed here for a fee.

www.manchester.gov.uk/info/448/archives-and-local-history
  Manchester Archives and Local History.
www.nationalarchives.co.uk All the available censuses can be viewed
  online for a fee (through the archives' collaborative partners
  www.findmypast.co.uk and www.ancestry.co.uk).
www.thegenealogist.co.uk All the available censuses can be accessed
  here for a fee.

Addresses
The National Archives
Kew
Richmond
Surrey
TW9 4DU

Manchester Archives and Local History
Central Library
St Peter's Square
City Centre
M2 5PD

The People's History Museum
The Pump House
Bridge Street
Manchester
M3 3 ER

CHAPTER 4

'Coal and Canals Polished Them Off'

Focus on History: The Dangers of Industrial Towns
Key source: Local Newspapers

Local and national newspapers are a valuable resource for family history and never more so since the fantastic resource The British Newspaper Archive became available online (www.britishnewspaperarchive.co.uk). This currently holds over eight million scanned newspaper pages dating from 1710 to 1959, and more pages from more publications are being added all the time. But don't forget also that real and significant clippings from newspapers often turn up among family papers. You may also find newspapers from the past lining the drawers in old furniture, or wrapping objects that have found their way into the attic. If you immerse yourself in any local newspaper from the past, you will immediately understand far more about your ancestor's life in a particular town than you might have done by virtually any other means. Newspaper articles may includes reports of events (for example, charity bazaars, or the openings of schools and hospitals) in which your ancestors are named because they were directly involved. And, if, in the course of your family history research, you discover that any of your ancestors died in unusual circumstances, you should always consider looking for reports of their deaths (and the inquests into them) in the local newspaper. Journalists' accounts turn facts into stories, and transform the names on your family tree into real people who were active members of a community.

The Stories
When, as a child, I asked any member of my mother's family about our Lancashire ancestors, he or she would look at me grimly, remind me how lucky I was to live on a modern housing estate in a leafy suburb and talk about how 'coal and canals' had been the death of our ancestors. I didn't

A Wigan miner in the 1890s – the squatting position was commonly adopted even above ground. (With thanks to Ron Hunt)

have to delve too far back into the family tree to find out that these morbid pronouncements were based on some awful truths. Death certificates provided me with the bare facts about those who had met their end in the mines and the waterways of Lancashire. But it was only when I turned to local newspapers that these events became explicable in terms of the surrounding industrial environment and the general tone of life in the local community.

The Cost of Coal

In the nineteenth century, Wigan was a small but rapidly-expanding industrial town well within what was to become the vast industrial and urban belt connecting Liverpool and Manchester. By 1899, the town had a population of 60,000. Coal and cotton created an interdependent economy, providing much of the town's employment and indirectly funding all the other business in the town. In the second half of the nineteenth century, there were as many as 1,000 pit shafts within five miles of Wigan town centre. Because of its plentiful underground coal reserves, the town was known as the area of 'black diamond fields'.

Cannel

One branch of the Lancashire coal industry was the mining of cannel, or 'parrot coal' which burned with a particularly bright and noisy flame and which was used in the making of gas. Ornaments, candlesticks and sugar boxes made of polished cannel graced the mantelpieces of many of my Wigan relatives.

Running my eye down any of the nineteenth-century censuses as they related to my family, I saw that a great many of the men worked in the Wigan coalmines in one capacity or another: as 'drawers', pony drivers' and 'firemen'. The majority, though, were 'hewers' – a tough occupation involving scooping out the coal with a pick and crowbar. Life would have been hard for these men who were paid according to how much coal they extracted each week.

Throughout the nineteenth century, more than a thousand miners a year died in Britain. Among them, unfortunately, were two of my great-great-grandfathers. The first, Benjamin Wilkinson, was killed on 3 February 1873 at the age of 53. His death certificate states that he died due to a fall of roof and that he 'lived a few minutes'. I wondered whether

Miners at the Wigan Coal and Iron Company, 1890s. (With thanks to Ron Hunt)

I could find out more. In the local library, I looked through microfilm copies of the *Wigan Observer and District Advertiser*, for the week just after Benjamin's death and found an item on 8 February 1873 relating to

THE WIGAN OBSE

HINDLEY.

COLLIERY ACCIDENTS.—On Saturday Mr. C. E. Driffield held an inquest at the Derby Arms, Hindley, on the body of Joseph Wood, aged 47 years, of Bridgewater-street. The deceased had worked at the Springs Colliery, Hindley Green, as dataller, when a stone fell from the roof and so injured his back that he died on Jan. 30th. Verdict, "Accidental death."— On Monday, Benjamin Wilkinson, aged 53 years, of Market-street, was at work in the Deep Pit, Hindley Colliery, when a quantity of "buzzard" fell from the roof and so injured him that he expired before he was got home. An inquest was held at the Bear's Paw, on Wednesday, when a verdict of "Accidentally killed" was returned. Deceased leaves a wife and nine children to mourn his loss.

(left column fragment) ro essays Tuesday e Green- r, and an ent. The d was on er was on After a through, interest- otted to ally con- titutions, ge. He tocracy,

(right column fragment) BREA police c summor Blundel Mr. W(and sta terferen ordered Loc Board near th preside Lamb, Thomp and Co was in plans,

This report on the death of my great-great grandfather Benjamin Wilkinson appeared in the *Wigan Observer and District Advertiser* in 1873.

Transcript of newspaper report on 8 February 1873

On Monday, Benjamin Wilkinson aged 53 years, of Market Street, was at work in the Deep Pit, Hindley Colliery, when a quantity of buzzard fell from the roof and so injured him that he expired before he got home. An inquest was held at the Bear's Paw, on Wednesday, when a verdict of 'Accidentally Killed' was returned. Deceased leaves a wife and nine children to mourn his loss.

(From the microfiche of the *Wigan Observer and District Advertiser* on 8 February 1873. Thanks to Mr P. M. Ogden)

the colliery accident in question. It contains some telling detail. First, Benjamin died in the ominously named 'Deep Pit' at Hindley Colliery. Secondly he was killed by a fall of 'buzzard' and did not die immediately, but 'before he got home'. Suddenly the bare facts on the certificate took on life. After the accident, Benjamin, it said, was 'carried home' (rather than – interestingly – to somewhere where he might have received medical attention), but he didn't make it. The newspaper report also gives the human angle on the story – Benjamin left a wife and nine children. I was able to speculate what effects his death might have had on them.

A second great-great-grandfather of mine, James Cooke, was also a Lancashire miner. He worked from boyhood as a hewer at No. 1 Crawford Pit which belonged to the Wigan Coal and Iron Company. This was a massive enterprise employing approximately 10,000 men. James's death certificate records that he died because of a 'roof fall' in September 1884. Again, I managed to flesh out the story a little by searching a microfilm copy of the *Wigan Observer and District Advertiser* for the week after his death. Unlike Benjamin, James, I learned, died at the scene of the accident and left a wife and four children.

The dirtiest job in the world: miners hewing coal, Wigan 1890s. (With thanks to Ron Hunt)

Miners hauling up a tub of coal. (With thanks to Ron Hunt)

FATAL ACCIDENT AT ASPULL.

On Wednesday, at the Crown Inn, Aspull, Mr. Edge, coroner, held an inquest touching the death of James Cooke, a miner, 42 years of age, who resided at Ivy Brow, Aspull, and who lost his life through a fall of roof at the No. 1 Crawford Pit, belonging to the Wigan Coal and Iron Co. It seemed that on Monday morning he was engaged at his work in the mine when a portion of the roof suddenly fell upon him and completely buried him. He was extricated as soon as possible, but was found to be quite dead. The deceased leaves a wife and four children. Mr. Webster was present at the enquiry on behalf of the company. The jury returned a verdict of "Accidentally killed," no blame being attached to anyone.

The report in the *Wigan Observer and District Advertiser* on the inquest into the death of James Cooke, 1884.

Transcript of newspaper report: Saturday, 20 September 1884.

FATAL COLLIERY ACCIDENT - On Wednesday, at the Crown Inn, Aspull, Mr Edge coroner, held an inquest touching the death of James Cooke, a miner, 42 years of age, who resided at Ivy Brow, Aspull, and who lost his life through a fall of roof at the No. 1 Crawford Pit, belonging to the Wigan Coal and Iron Company. It seemed that on Monday morning he was engaged at his work in the mine when a portion of the roof suddenly fell upon him and completely buried him. He was extricated as soon as possible, but was found to be quite dead. The deceased leaves a wife and four children. Mr Webster was present at the inquiry on behalf of the company. The jury returned a verdict of 'accidentally killed.'

(From the microfiche of the *Wigan Observer and District Advertiser* on 20 September 1884. Thanks to Mr P.M. Ogden)

The Curse of the Canals

If you weren't killed in the pit in nineteenth-century Wigan, it seems that you were likely to meet your end in one of the canals. The Leeds-Liverpool canal was part of the reason for Wigan's prosperous industrial economy since it connected the town with Leeds, Liverpool and Manchester. Unfortunately three ancestors of mine were to meet their end in its grimy depths.

> ## Dead in the Water
>
> Drowning was an all too common feature of life in industrial towns in the nineteenth century. Canals and rivers could be death-traps in more ways than one. Local waterways proved a popular repository for unwanted babies (some aborted, and some the victims of infanticide), and there was a significant rise in the number of suicides by drowning in Britain in the last quarter of the nineteenth century. Towpaths, which ran beside pubs and hostelries, were often unpaved and slippery late at night; they provided a conveniently ill-lit venue for drunken fights, robberies and muggings.

The first of these was my great-great-great-grandfather, Enoch Fletcher. He drowned in February 1869. The registrar who filled out his death certificate did nothing to save the family's embarrassment by adding a note with an unspoken a moral undertone, 'fell in accidentally while intoxicated'. A record of the inquest into Enoch's death appeared a few days later in *The Wigan Observer and District Advertiser*.

Newspaper reports like this can give you enough information to set your imagination alight. The description of Enoch as 'quite dead when taken out' of the canal caused me to speculate on the recovery process. Drowned bodies, in the first instance, apparently drop to the bottom of canals. If the weather is cold, as I am sure it was in Wigan that February,

Busy with barges: the Leeds-Liverpool canal, Wigan, in the 1890s. (With thanks to Ron Hunt)

The report in the *Wigan Observer and District Advertiser* on the drowning of Enoch Fletcher in 1869.

Transcript of Newspaper report: Saturday, 20 February 1869

CASE OF DROWNING - An inquest was held at the house of Mr Nathan Tyrer, Commercial Inn, near Top Lock, Aspull on Tuesday last, by F. Price Esq., deputy coroner for the district, on the body of Enoch Fletcher, engine fitter, employed at the Wigan Coal and Iron Company's Works. Deceased fell into the canal on Saturday evening, near the Top Lock, and was quite dead when taken out. He was 54 years of age, and leaves a wife and family. A verdict of 'accidentally drowned while intoxicated' was returned by the jury.

(From the microfiche of the *Wigan Observer and District Advertiser*. Thanks to Mr P. M. Ogden)

they can remain below for some time. Enoch's body would probably have been raised to the surface with a 'keb' – or iron rake – normally used to retrieve coal and other articles from the canal bed. His swollen corpse would then have been brought back to the Commercial Inn – probably the place where he had his last-ever drink – for identification and for the inquest.

I wondered how common it was to drown from intoxication in nineteenth-century Wigan in the latter half of the nineteenth century. The local trade directory – *Wigan Directory* (1869), published in the same year that Enoch died – alerted me to the fact that the Commercial Inn was one of 139 public houses, sixty-two beer houses and eight breweries in the town. A lot of men (and women too) probably stumbled home dangerously drunk at around that time. Scanning the death columns of the papers, I realised that many people did indeed meet a similar fate. But, I was hardly prepared for the fact that among them would be another relation of mine from the same generation – my great-great-great-grandfather, Lawrence Cooke.

'COAL AND CANALS POLISHED THEM OFF'

Lawrence was a 77-year-old cotton spinner and journeyman, who drowned in the Westwood Park area of Wigan again in the Leeds-Liverpool canal on 3 September 1881. His death certificate says simply, 'Found Drowned'. I have since learned that this phrase was a convenient catch-all for a multitude of possible circumstances of death in the late nineteenth century – it simply means that the body was found in water. It is believed that official statistics at the time grossly underestimated the actual amount of suicide, murder, manslaughter and infanticide occurring. Open verdicts were often returned in the case of adults who had died under suspicious circumstances, especially those fished out of canals or rivers.

A Knife and An Apple

As a family historian, there is nothing that gives you quite as much of a thrill as finding out what was in the pockets of your own ancestor on the night he or she died.

In Lawrence's case, the newspaper account of the death yielded a delightful fragment of information. When his pockets were searched – presumably in order to identify him – they yielded two items: 'a knife and an apple'. These seemed to me to be particularly expressive reminders of a simple life suddenly curtailed. An image of Lawrence was suddenly before me – a man of simple practicality – a man who prudently took an apple and a knife with him when he went out. And of course, the fact that there had apparently been no money in Lawrence's pockets allowed me to speculate that he might have been robbed and then murdered in the park on his last journey home. Perhaps he had simply been unable to get to his knife in time . . . .

I'll never know the real reason why Lawrence Cooke died. Inspired by his story (and that of Enoch) I did a little more research into drowning and discovered that he would have been lying face down in the water with his head hanging and it is likely that his corpse would have been bruised and discoloured. Nowadays, it is possible to tell from forensic tests whether a drowned person stopped breathing before or after they entered the water, but in the nineteenth century, it would have been difficult, if not impossible, to ascertain whether Lawrence's injuries were the result of buffeting by the water, or by injuries sustained before death.

The Poignancy of an Umbrella

To lose four members of the family to what might loosely be termed 'industrial accidents' seems unlikely, to lose five seems highly irresponsible! The fifth member of my family to lose her life was my great-great-great aunt, Margaret Daniels, 'a factory hand' (according to her death certificate). Margaret drowned on 8 March 1874, 'above No. 8 Lock, Upper Ince' at the tender age of just twelve. The Deputy Registrar for Wigan, William Henry Milligan, was obviously so fascinated by the detail of the Coroner's Report of the drowning that he filled in the space accorded to 'Cause of Death' on Margaret's death certificate, with far more detail than was customary. The record reads: 'Drowned in canal. Passing along bank in evening carrying umbrella. Accident – in the water 2 days.'

Intrigued – particularly by the detail about the umbrella – I looked for the record of the death in the *Wigan Examiner*. Again, I was delighted to find that a report appeared later that week and it included some extra gruesome details (see the actual report on p.6.

Margaret had met her brother on the night she died. Why, I wondered, was that event considered significant enough to be recorded in the newspaper? Why had he failed to protect her from whatever later befell her? Who were the two men whom Margaret had followed down the canal bank? Evidently the journalist thought that they were significant enough to warrant a mention. And the umbrella is mentioned again. Why is that? Is the journalist suggesting that Margaret used it to try to defend herself against potential attackers? Was she still clutching that umbrella after she entered the water, or was it thrown in after her? Did the men use it against her in their attack? The newspaper account set my mind reeling: it seemed such a shame that a girl who took the time and care to take an umbrella out with her in the evening should have ended up dying.

The newspaper accounts of these deaths, however brief, have both animated and given substance to the facts about these five ancestors. They died so close together in time and in such close geographical proximity, that I could not help but be impressed and chastened by the dangerous texture of life in nineteenth-century Wigan.

Key Source: Local Newspapers

Although some provincial newspapers came into existence in the eighteenth century, they tended to cover national and international rather than local news. Over the course of the nineteenth century, these papers (and the many others that joined them) took on more of a local focus.

Local newspapers proliferated after the reduction of stamp duty (tax on each sheet of paper used) in 1836 and its abolition in 1855.

Whilst the activities of the rich and famous had always been discussed in newspapers, it was only in the late nineteenth and twentieth centuries that the activities of ordinary people came to seem newsworthy. At the beginning, these were confined to mentions in descriptions of significant local events, and the rulings of local Quarter and Petty Sessions (courts). As time went on, the number of different reasons why your ancestor might have appeared in a newspaper increased.

How do I find relevant local newspapers?
The best online resource for historic newspapers is the British Newspaper Archive (www.britishnewspaperarchive.co.uk). This is the result of a collaboration between the British Library and Findmypast. The lives of your ancestors and the events in their localities can potentially be discovered (for a fee) using keywords, names, location, dates or newspaper title. The project began by covering late eighteenth- and nineteenth-century newspapers with a focus on those produced in big cities, especially London and those with a county circulation. More and more papers are being added all the time, with a new emphasis on those from the twentieth century.

If your ancestors hailed from a small village, or provincial town, it is likely that the local newspapers will not (yet) have been digitised. Actual newspapers (and in many cases the microfilms of them), however, can be found in a number of places:

• Local History and Local Studies Libraries
• County Record Offices
• The British Library Newspaper Library. Print newspapers are now stored at the National Newspaper Library, Boston Spa (see full address below); digitised and microfiche copies can be viewed at The British Library Newsroom, London (see full address below).

The problem with using newspapers that have not been digitised and put online as a family history resource is that – in most cases – you need already to know the date (or approximate date) of the event that you are looking for. For example, if you have a death certificate stating that your great-grandmother died in a house fire on 10 March 1878, you should look in copies of the local newspaper for the days immediately following this. Bear in mind that many local newspapers were published only weekly or fortnightly, however.

Some libraries hold indexes to their newspapers that record the important names mentioned in individual articles, others hold indexes to the subjects covered. You should always find out what aids to research exist before visiting the library.

What can I find out from local newspapers?
In addition to giving you a general feel for life in a community, newspapers may specifically include:

- birth, marriage and death announcements (as in today's newspapers these by no means cover the lives of everybody in a community)
- obituaries
- items on significant local disasters, fires, train crashes, epidemics or mining accidents
- accounts of inquests
- reports of bazaars, charity concerts or fundraising events which mention the name of your ancestors
- adverts for shops and businesses
- details about the sale of farms and businesses
- police notices
- announcements about the sailing of ships
- accounts of court proceedings
- accounts of significant local council meetings
- notices of bankruptcies.

Think laterally
Before beginning a search of local newspapers, it is worth finding out from the local library how many newspapers a town had in the past and how regularly they were published. Make sure that you check all the papers. In addition to the *Wigan Examiner* and *Wigan Observer and District Advertiser* (mentioned in this chapter), there were, for example, many newspapers in Wigan at various times during the nineteenth century including the *Wigan Gazette*, *Wigan Herald*, *Wigan Journal*, *Wigan Mirror*, *Wigan Standard*, *Wigan Star and Advertiser* and the *Wigan Times*.

It is worth remembering that unless they had benefited from the Education Act of 1870 (which began the process of making primary education compulsory), many of our ancestors would have been unable to read the local newspaper. Lydia Cooke (the subject of Chapter 2), for instance, would have been unable to read the account of her husband James's death in the pit in 1884.

If you are looking for an event that took place in a region or local town but was of national importance and if you are unsure of the date, you could consult *Palmer's Index to the Times (1790-1905)*; *The Official Index to the Times (1906-1980)* or *Palmer's Full Text Online (1785-1870)* which are available on CD Rom at many libraries. These will tell you when the event was reported in the *Times* newspaper. You can then investigate your local newspaper records armed with the correct date.

Resources to Take You Further
Books
Arnot, Chris, *Britain's Lost Mines: The Vanished Kingdom of the Men Who Carved Out the Nation's Wealth*, Aurum Press, 2013.
Chapman, Colin R., *An Introduction to Using Newspapers and Periodicals*, Federation of Family History Societies, 1993.
Gibson, J., Langston B., and Smith, B. W., *Local Newspapers, 1750-1920, England and Wales, Channel Islands, and the Isle of Man, a Select Location List*, 2nd ed, Federation of Family History Societies, 2002.
Hadfield. Charles, *British Canals: An Illustrated History*, David and Charles, 1974.
Maw, Peter, *Transport and the Industrial City: Manchester and the Canal Age, 1750-1850*, Manchester University Press, 2013.
McLaughlin, E., *Family History from Newspapers*, Family Tree Magazine, 1994.
Times, The, *The Tercentenary Handlist of English and Welsh Newspapers, Magazines and Reviews, 1620-1919*, Time Publishing Co., 1920 (Dawson Reprint, 1966).
Tonks, David, *My Ancestor was a Coalminer*, Society of Genealogists' Enterprises Ltd, 2003.
Wigan Directory, J. Worral, 1869 (reprinted Neil Richardson, 1983).

Websites

www.britishnewspaperarchive.co.uk Digitised pages of many national and regional newspapers from 1710 to 1963.

www.bl.uk British Library.

www.cmhrc.pwp.blueyonder.co.uk Coal Mining History Resource Centre.

This includes a National Database of over 200,000 Mining Deaths and Injuries between 1840 and 1970.

www.discovery.nationalarchives.gov.uk/results/r?_q=coal+mining+records

Coal Mining Records in the National Archives.

www.dmm.org.uk Durham Mining Museum.

This provides some general information for family historians wishing to trace ancestors who were miners, including for example, details of shafts, mines, mine managers and abandoned mines.

www.mikeclarke.myzen.co.uk/2010%20Historical%20Character.pdf The Historical Character of English Canals and Its Conservation.

www.ncm.org.uk. National Coal Mining Museum for England. Over 5,000 books on mining history are collected here.

www.penninewaterways.co.uk Pennine Waterways (includes lots of photographs).

http://www1.rhbnc.ac.uk/sociopolitical-science/vrp/Findings/rfarcher.PDF

'Violence in the North-West with Special Reference to Liverpool and Manchester, 1850-1914'. A Paper by the Economic and Social Research Council.

www.scottishminingmuseum.com Scottish Mining Museum.

www.shropshiremines.org.uk/ Shropshire Mines Trust.

www.wales-underground.org.uk/ National Mining Museum of Wales.

www.wiganworld.co.uk Website on history of Wigan.

Addresses

National Mining Museum of Wales
Blaenafon
Torfaen
Newport NP4 9XP

The British Library Newsroom
The British Library
96, Euston Road
London NW1 2DB
Durham Mining Museum
c/o Spennymore Town Council
Town Hall
Spennymore
County Durham
DL16 6DG

National Newspaper Library
The British Library
Boston Spa
Wetherby
West Yorkshire
LS23 7BQ

The National Coal Mining Museum for England
Caphouse Colliery
New Road
Overton
Wakefield
WF4 4RH

Scottish Mining Museum
Lady Victoria Colliery
Newtongrange
Midlothian
EH22 4QN

CHAPTER 5

'Daddy Saw It All'

Focus on History: The Second World War
Key Source: Diaries

You should always bear in mind what was happening in the wider world when researching the lives of your ancestors. Many of them will have lived through important historical events – wars, coronations, cotton famines, epidemics and floods to name but a few. Some of these will have affected their lives deeply. Occasionally you may come across a real gem – a first-hand account of a particular historical event through which you can almost 'hear' your ancestor's distinct personality. This might be in the form of a letter, or a memoir, or – more likely – a diary. Unlike birth, marriage and death certificates, and indeed census returns, diaries make the past dynamic: in their pages the characters from the family tree are once again in action. A diary, unlike virtually any other source, gives a first-hand account to set alongside textbook versions of what life was like for people living in the past.

My father, William Symes, as a young boy. Photographed in Blackpool c. 1938. (Author's collection)

The Story

It is every researcher's dream to find a journal written by a family member. Even the scantiest detail jotted in an appointments' diary can be highly revealing of the life and times of its owner. But, in the case of the little black leather book found in a cardboard box in the attic, the reward was much richer. Not only did this pocket schoolboy diary tell me a great deal about the life of its writer – my own father – but it also gave me a graphic day-by-day account of one of the most important events in British history, the May Blitz on Liverpool during the Second World War.

Liverpool Targetted

In the mid twentieth-century, the city of Liverpool (together with Birkenhead), was Britain's largest west-coast port. During the Second World War, it was a prime target for the Germans because of its huge dock system and the fact that it was the main link between Britain and the USA – the place where food, fuel, raw materials, weapons and troops entered the country. Outside London, Liverpool was Hitler's main British target which is why between August 1940 and January 1942, the Luftwaffe made about eighty air raids on Merseyside.

1941 was the year that my father, William Symes, an only child, turned thirteen. His father was the manager of a branch of Freeman, Hardy and Willis in the central suburb of Walton, Liverpool and the family lived above the shop. Eighteen months before he started his diary, my father had suffered the ordeal of evacuation to North Wales. Now, back with his parents, and living just where Hitler most wanted to drop a bomb, he was determined to keep an account of what was going on.

My father wrote the diary whilst living here at 1 County Road, Liverpool, above the Freeman, Hardy and Willis shoe shop then managed by his father. Photograph from 1973. (With thanks to Roger Hull at Liverpool Record Office)

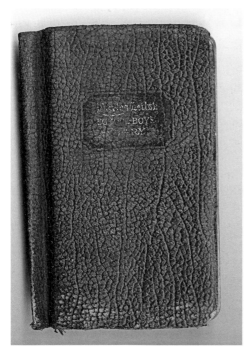

The unexciting front cover of my father's diary belied its hidden treasures. (Author's collection)

Letts Diaries, one of the most reputable diary publishers, was established in 1812, when the stationer John Letts combined a calendar and a journal. This diary came in three different formats according to how much pocket money you had. My father bought the two-shilling option, a fact which perhaps gives away his lower middle-class status as the only son of the manager of a Freeman, Hardy and Willis shoe shop. Public schoolboys and undergraduates were offered a choice of more expensive diaries. The quality and type of diary can be a good indicator of your ancestor's class status. (Author's collection)

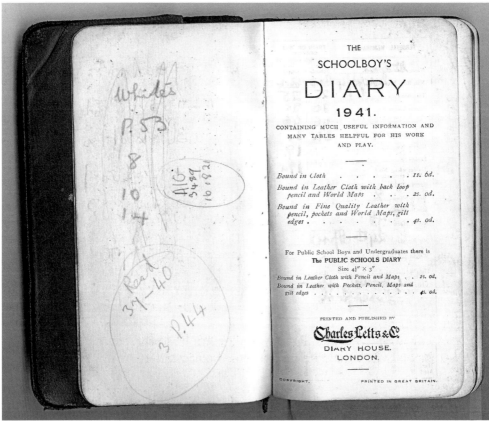

Public News and Private Thoughts

My father was intelligent and sensitive, but like many young boys, he didn't give vent to his feelings directly in the diary. The entries are unemotional, but they are moving because of the way the information is arranged: on every page, details of everyday life are mixed up with the horrific details of war. In the entries for January 1941, for example, he reported on the icy weather, the fact that the taps at home were frozen and that he had been 'hit in the eye by a snowball' in the school playground. But at the same time, he kept a daily count of the number of air-raids and air-raid warnings affecting Liverpool. The number and ferocity of these makes frightening reading. A typical entry is that for Saturday 15 February 1941, which reads 'One short afternoon raid. One short evening raid. One raid from 12 midnight till 2.30am. Guns, planes and bombs heard. [3R].' The '[3R]' is my father's code for the number of air-raids there were each day. A series of similar entries close together shows just how persistent the raids were and how terrifying it must have been for a young boy.

> Thursday 9 January 1941. 'Pretty Heavy Raid, 7.30pm – 1.30am. [R]'
> Friday 10 January. 'Long Warning 8pm-12pm. No Guns or Planes Heard. [4R]'
> Monday 13 January. 'Heavy Gunfire 8.15pm – 11.30pm. [R]'
> Wednesday 15 January. 'Two, short, quiet night raids. [2R]'

There was no pattern to what my father chose to record each day. The only certainties were that he always wrote something and that the entries were all short and to the point. Often he jotted down the latest war news, the progress of the Allies, the deaths of European leaders, the advance of Hitler, and Churchill's speeches on the radio. On Monday 20 January, for example, he recorded that President Roosevelt had been inaugurated and on Thursday 30 January, that 'The British Captured Derna Today (N. Africa). Rumanian Riots Stopped'. But, with equal meticulousness, he also wrote down the detail of his boyish hobbies: the games of billiards he played with his father, the recorder his mother gave him for his birthday, the gramophone records he listened to with his uncle, the treacle he ate at his aunt's, games of dominoes and cricket and the proud fact that he had managed to make a 'Hawker Hurricane plane in Meccano'.

Life at school was different from how it had been before the war. Assemblies were held in unaccustomed places; there were 'gas mask

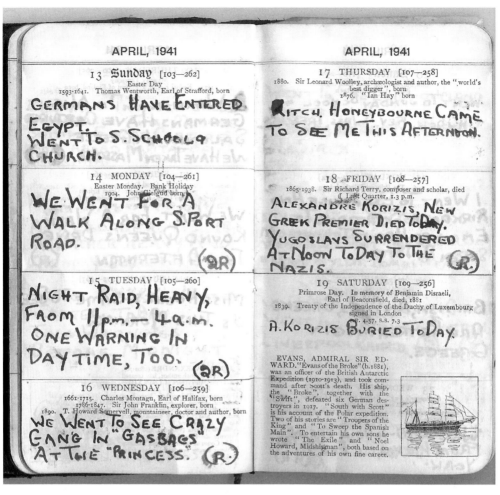

APRIL, 1941

APRIL, 1941

13 **Sunday** [103—262]
Easter Day
1593-1641. Thomas Wentworth, Earl of Strafford, born

GERMANS HAVE ENTERED
EGYPT.
WENT TO S. SCHOOL &
CHURCH.

17 THURSDAY [107—258]
1880. Sir Leonard Woolley, archæologist and author, the "world's
best digger", born
1876. "Ian Hay" born

RITCH. HONEYBOURNE CAME
TO SEE ME THIS AFTERNOON.

14 MONDAY [104—261]
Easter Monday. Bank Holiday
1904. John Gielgud born

WE WENT FOR A
WALK ALONG S.PORT
ROAD.
(2R)

18 FRIDAY [108—257]
1865-1938. Sir Richard Terry, composer and scholar, died
(Last Quarter, 1.3 p.m.

ALEXANDRE KORIZIS, NEW
GREEK PREMIER DIED TODAY.
YUGOSLAVS SURRENDERED
AT NOON TODAY TO THE (R.)
NAZIS.

15 TUESDAY [105—260]

NIGHT RAID, HEAVY,
FROM 11 p.m.— 4 a.m.
ONE WARNING IN
DAY TIME, TOO.
(2R)

19 SATURDAY [109—256]
Primrose Day. In memory of Benjamin Disraeli,
Earl of Beaconsfield, died, 1881
1839. Treaty of the Independence of the Duchy of Luxembourg
signed in London
R. 4.57, S.S. 7.3

A. KORIZIS BURIED TODAY.

16 WEDNESDAY [106—259]
1661-1715. Charles Montagu, Earl of Halifax, born
1786-1847. Sir John Franklin, explorer, born
1890. T. Howard Somervell, mountaineer, doctor and author, born

WE WENT TO SEE CRAZY
GANG IN "GASBAGS"
AT THE "PRINCESS". (R.)

EVANS, ADMIRAL SIR ED-
WARD. "Evans of the Broke" (b.1881),
was an officer of the British Antarctic
Expedition (1910-1913), and took com-
mand after Scott's death. His ship,
the "Broke", together with the
"Swift", defeated six German destroyers in 1917. "South with Scott"
is his account of the Polar expedition.
Two of his stories are "Troupers of the
King" and "To Sweep the Spanish
Main". To entertain his own sons he
wrote "The Exile" and "Noel
Howard, Midshipman", both based on
the adventures of his own fine career.

Diary entries can be an interesting mixture of the public and the private. Many diarists write – at least partly – in code. Here my father records how many air-raids [R] have taken place each night. Pre-printed information in a diary can be very revealing of the times in which it was published. Here the birthdates of famous Britons are recorded. The diary is suggesting role models to whom the diarist ought to aspire. The weekly biographies of famous people are included for a reason. Admiral Evans is here because he 'defeated six German destroyers in 1917'. He is thus a fitting hero for a diary printed during the Second World War and designed to raise morale. (Author's collection)

practices' and visits to the school air-raid shelter. Occasionally, the detail is chilling in its starkness. On Tuesday 18 March, my father wrote, 'Mr Whitehouse, one of our masters, who was killed in last Wednesday's Raid, was buried this afternoon'. And two days later on Thursday 20 March, he observed, as if he had almost forgotten the reason, 'We had [a] new master for English'. At home and in the neighbourhood, things were different too. On Tuesday 18 February, 1941 there was a Fire Bomb Meeting 'for our block held in [the] Scotch Wool Store'. From March onwards, my grandfather took a regular turn at the fire watch.

Amongst all the uncertainty and terror, there were still some pleasures, visits to the Astoria and Princess cinemas, for example, to see films such as 'Mad About Music' with Deanna Durbin and 'Keep your Seats Please', with George Formby and Florence Desmond. And the family also went to the Empire Theatre to see Arthur Askey in 'Variety'. Occasionally, my father and his parents managed to escape from Liverpool for a few days to other places, such as Stalybridge and York, where they had relations. Ironically on the visit to York in April (Sat 26th) the diary stated that 'Liverpool was raided and so was York [L:R], [Y:R]'

It was in May 1941 that the situation in Liverpool became intolerable. Between 1 and 7 May, the city suffered its worst raids in the infamous May Blitz. My father, of course, did not know exactly what was going on: all he knew was that many familiar streets had been hit and that neighbours wanted to share the family air-raid shelter. He recorded the night of Saturday 3 May in his diary like this: 'Worst raid yet 10.30pm – 2.30am. Index Street, Carisbrooke Road, Royal Street, Lind Street. All Cars [ie trams] stopped. Mr and Mrs Cross in shelter.' On Thursday 8 May, the Cross family took the Symeses to the nearby town of Warrington to stay with a relation of theirs for safety. As luck would have it, Warrington too was raided that night and Liverpool three times: '[W:1, L3]'.

The May Blitz on Liverpool, 1941
By the end of the first week of May, 681 planes had dropped 870 tonnes of high explosives and over 112,000 incendiaries, 1,746 people were killed, 1,154 people seriously injured, and 76,000 people were made homeless. On 3 May, generally recognised as the worst night of the Blitz, the cargo ship *Malakand* was hit and exploded in Huskisson Dock.

After the May Blitz, my grandparents realised that it was too dangerous for the family to stay in Liverpool city centre at night. On Monday 26 May 1941, my father recorded, 'Mam went [. . .] looking for sleeping room in Aughton. She found one at a farm. We go there on Wednesday.' Aughton was an agricultural village on the railway line north of Liverpool towards Ormskirk. Two days later on Wednesday 28 May, my father recorded his relief at getting out of the city. 'We went by electric train with dad to the room on the farm at Aughton.' From this point onwards, the Symes family travelled to the farm to sleep nearly every night for the rest of 1941.

The Diary and The Family Tree
When researching a family tree, a diary can be useful because it reveals information about family members other than the writer him or herself. The diary told me a lot about my grandparents, my grandfather who sometimes stayed behind in the shoe shop in Liverpool to do his bookkeeping whilst his wife and child went to Aughton, and my brave grandmother who remained stoical throughout food and clothes rationing. I found out more too about distant family members, the aunt in York who, marvellously, could drive and had her own car, the uncle who ran a milk business and upon whose float my father would sometimes ride, and the relations in Canada who sent supportive letters every so often. Their addresses are all there at the back of the diary as well, including the exact house numbers and street names of people for whom previously I had only had the name of a town.

As well as giving his life shape and colour, my father's diary enable me to answer several pressing questions about the family tree. I had, for example, previously searched in vain for the birth certificate of my father's Aunty Jenny because I was unsure about the exact year in which she had been born. As luck would have it, however, my father had recorded the birthdays (and ages) of many of his relatives in his diary. In March 1941 he recorded his Aunty Jenny's birthday. Because of this entry, I was able narrow down my search for the record of Jenny's birth to the relevant quarter of the correct year (1890) in the online Birth Index (at ancestry.co.uk), and then finally to obtain the birth certificate. Diaries can be similarly helpful in recording the dates of family marriages, deaths, baptisms and funerals. Even if you already know these dates from the certificates in your possession, there is a certain satisfaction and excitement in having a diary's corroboration of the facts, plus, of course, potentially a description of the event.

The very last entry in my father's diary on Wednesday 31 December

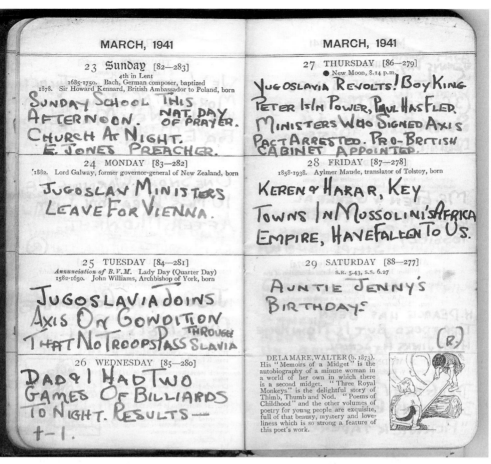

The entry for Saturday 29 March 1941 helped me in the search for my great aunt's birth certificate. (Author's collection)

stated: 'Mam and I went to town this afternoon. I bought a 1942 diary and a book.' I am just hoping that one day I will be able to lay my hands on that next diary!

Key Source: Diaries

A diary is a daily record, written on the day of the events it describes, or very soon after. Unlike autobiographies or memoirs, which are crafted into full texts at a later date, diaries usually do not have the polish of professional writing. They are unique because they provide the writer's immediate reaction to what is going on in the world around him or her. For the purposes of family history research, the term 'diary' can cover a

85

Bomb damage in Liverpool after the May Blitz of 1941. On the left are the ruins of Lewis's department store. (With thanks to Roger Hull at Liverpool Record Office)

multitude of types of record including: travel diaries, military diaries, letter-books (in which letters to friends are copied out to provide an ongoing record), scrapbooks and pocketbooks. In practice the terms 'diary' and 'journal' are used interchangeably.

Very few diaries were written by members of the working classes before the Education Act of 1870 came closer to making elementary schooling compulsory. It was only in the twentieth century, with the rapid increase in popular literacy, that the art of diary writing became accessible to all social classes. Major world events such as the First and Second World Wars also encouraged many to put pen to paper to record their experiences.

Where am I likely to find diaries written by my ancestors?
If you are not lucky enough to come across a diary among your family papers,

- try www.discovery.nationalarchives.gov.uk. This is a portal to 32 million descriptions of records held by the National Archives and in more than

2,500 archives across the country. Content can be searched by keyword and narrowed down by time period. Some nine million records, including many diaries, have been digitised and can be viewed online. Alternatively, you may discover the location of diaries (as yet not digitised) which you can then view in person at local or county archives or at the National Archives itself. Make sure that you contact the relevant archive well in advance and book an appointment to view the diary in question: many records will be stored in strong rooms and take time to retrieve

• bear in mind that collections of diaries of particular types can be found in specialist archives, for example, The Mass Observation archive (www.massobs.org.uk) at the University of Sussex includes many diaries written by people during the Second World War

• an ongoing project to digitise diaries kept by soldiers during the First World War can be accessed at www.operationwardiary.org – with many of the diaries so far digitised available through www.discovery.national archives.gov.uk

• as well as older material, some more modern diaries are also held in archives. Be aware that the Data Protection Act may prevent public access to personal information that is under 75 years old. A depositor may also close the diary to public access until a specified time period has elapsed.

What can I find out about my ancestor from a diary?
A diary of any substance will enable you to 'hear' your ancestor's distinct voice or personality. If you are lucky it will contain a combination of facts and feelings. As well as telling you more about the personalities and activities of individual family members, it may record how the family experienced important historical events. A diary might also:

• mention family members previously unknown
• record significant dates (e.g. birthdays, dates of births, baptisms, marriages, deaths and burials)
• give the names of churches, chapels, schools or places of work
• detail periods of employment and illness
• provide leads to other sources of information (my father's diary, for example, refers to a newspaper article in which he is mentioned, letters, an autograph book, a drawing and a school magazine)
• contain an addresses section at the back which can enable you to trace living relatives.

Think laterally

Don't forget to look carefully at the pre-printed parts of a diary. My father's schoolboy diary included French and German verbs, logarithms and information about the metric system, scientific tables, information about careers and first aid, athletic records, pictures of aeroplane acrobatics and useful foreign phrases. All these will give you an idea of the sort of interests that a person like your ancestor was likely to have had.

Some pre-printed parts of a diary have blank sections for the writer to personalise. These can be very interesting to a family historian. Tables in my father's diary allowed him to fill in information about his life including: personal memoranda; train and bus services; pocket money; school timetables; presents he had been given; exam results; letters he had received and written; scores from cricket, football and hockey matches; and books he had read, borrowed, or lent, with a comment on each.

Title.	Author.	Remarks.	Title.	Author.	Remarks.
"O. Twist"	Dickens	Excellent	"William — The Outlaw"	Richmal Crompton	Excellent
"Black Beauty"	A. Sewell	Excellent	"William's Happy Days"	Richmal Crompton	Excellent.
"Off His Own Bat"	St. John Pearce	G.	"Just William"	Richmal Crompton	Excellent
"William — The Gangster"	Richmal Crompton	Excellent	"William — The Conqueror"	Richmal Crompton	Excellent.
"William — The Pirate"	Richmal Crompton	Excellent	"Ivanhoe"	Walter Scott	Excellent
"William — The Fourth"	Richmal Crompton	Excellent.	"Death In The Bubble"		Good.
"From Hand To Hand"	C. J. Hamilton	V.G.	"Sketches By Boz"	Charles Dickens	Excellent
			"Pickwick Papers"	Charles Dickens.	Excellent
"William"	Richmal Crompton	Excellent	"The Wizard Of The Woods"	Major C. Gilson	Good

My father's youthful taste in books is revealed. (Author's collection)

You may find all sorts of clues to your ancestors' lives between the pages of diaries. As well as pressed flowers and leaves, letters, and locks of hair, look out for newspaper cuttings, ticket stubs, postcards, photographs, restaurant and business cards, letters, pieces of maps, telegrams and pictures from magazines. Even a chocolate wrapper can give a clue to the way a life was lived!

Even if you don't find a diary by your immediate ancestor in an archive, you may find one by a more distant relative or at least by someone who lived in the same place at the same time, and who perhaps had the same sort of occupation. Reading their diaries could help you better to understand your own ancestor's life.

Resources to Take You Further
Books
Aughton, Peter, *Liverpool: A People's History*, Carnegie Publishing, 1990.
Ayers, Pat, *Liverpool Docklands*, Liver Press, 1999.
Batts, John Stuart, *British Manuscript Diaries of the Nineteenth Century: An Annotated Listing*, Rowman and Littlefield, 1976.
Broad, Richard and Fleming, Suzie (eds), *Nella Last's War: The Second World War Diaries of Housewife 49*, Profile Books, 2006.
Creaton, Heather, *Victorian Diaries: The Daily Lives of Victorian Men and Women*, Mitchell Beazley, 2001.
Garfield, Simon, *We Are At War: The Remarkable Diaries of Five Ordinary People in Extraordinary Times*, Ebury Press, 2006.
Matthews, William, *British Diaries: An Annotated Bibliography of British Diaries Written Between 1442 and 1942*, California UP, 1992.
Sheridan, Dorothy, *Wartime Women: A Mass-Observation Anthology of Women's Writings 1937-1945*, W&N, 2009.
Whittington-Egan, Richard, *The Great Liverpool Blitz*, The Gallery Press, 1987.

Websites
www.discovery.nationalarchives.gov.uk Portal to 32 million descriptions of records held by the National Archives and regional and local archives across the country.
www.iwm.org.uk/history/children-during-the-second-world-war Imperial War Museum's site describing children's experiences of the Second World War.

www.liverpool.gov.uk/libraries/archives-family-history/ Liverpool
    libraries and archives.
www.liverpoolmuseums.org.uk/mol/ Museum of Liverpool.
www.massobs.org.uk The Mass Observation Archive, recording
    everyday life in Britain.
www.old-merseytimes.co.uk/ Liverpool and Merseyside's life and times
    transcribed from old newspapers.
www.operationwardiary.org Ongoing project set up by the Imperial War
    Museum to digitise diaries of soldiers from the First World War.
www.streetsofliverpool.co.uk/ A pictorial history of Liverpool.
www.writinglives.org Writing Lives Project including an archive of
    digitised working-class writing from 1700 onwards.

Addresses
Liverpool Record Office
Central Library
William Brown Street
Liverpool
L3 8EW

Mass Observation Archive
The Keep,
Wollards Way
Brighton
BN1 9BP

Museum of Liverpool
Liverpool Waterfront
Pierhead
Liverpool
Liverpool
L3 1DG

CHAPTER 6

'She Had a Really Good Send Off'

Focus on History: Death and Burial
Key Source: Records Related to Death (particularly Obituaries)

A surprising number of bits of information connected with death turn up in family papers. You should treasure these, group them together and study them carefully. They may include anything from the obvious death certificates and grave plot certificates, to orders of service, funeral bills, mourning cards and newspaper obituaries. These documents are all, of course, interconnected. A death certificate may lead you on to an obituary, for example, and an obituary may lead you to a gravestone. The different sources simply tell the same story from a different angle. A funeral bill may detail what was provided at the funeral buffet; an order of service may inform you what hymns were sung and what words were said by whom. Think of these sources as the component parts that will allow you to build up the complete picture of your ancestor's final drama.

The Story
I recently found a piece of paper that might very easily have been thrown away years ago. It was the bill for the funeral of my great-grandmother, Elizabeth Symes in 1940.

I already knew from her death certificate that my great-grandmother died in Stalybridge, near Manchester, from 'cardiac failure, bronchitis and senile decay' in the spring of 1940. Her funeral bill, a photocopy of the original with a part annoyingly blanked out in the bottom left-hand corner, is nevertheless full of useful detail. It is, for instance, usefully headed with a reminder of her age – 84 –

My great-grandmother Elizabeth Symes (1855–1940) in 1928. (Author's collection)

Elizabeth Symes sitting on the doorstep of her son-in-law's temperance bar, Manchester, c 1924, surrounded by those who would mourn at her funeral. Back row: future daughter-in-law Alice Gillings (who became my grandmother); son-in-law Joe Mayo; daughter Emmie Mayo (née Symes); daughter Jenny Winstanley (née Symes); son Jack Symes (my grandfather); Elizabeth Symes (seated); granddaughter Marjorie Avison; granddaughter Elsie Winstanley. (Author's collection)

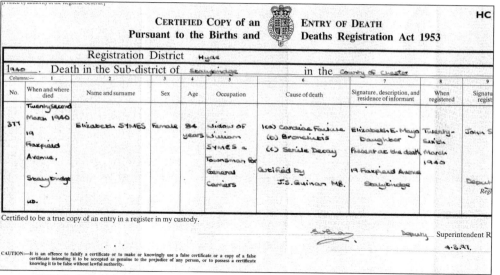

Elizabeth Symes's death certificate, 1940. (General Register Office)

and it is directed for the attention of the man who would settle the account, Elizabeth's son-in-law, Mr Mayo. The bill breaks down the costs of my great-grandmother's interment, from the price of the coffin, to the fee for not *one* but *two* mentions of the death in local newspapers (the *Manchester Evening News* and the *Stalybridge Reporter*). It didn't take me long to realise that Elizabeth's funeral was quite lavish for its times: £27, 7 shillings and 8 pence was no small amount to spend on a burial in the first year of the Second World War.

Elizabeth had led an impoverished early life. Born in Henstridge, Somerset in 1855, the daughter of an agricultural labourer and a glover, she had moved to Manchester to escape rural poverty in about 1880 and had worked – according to the 1891 census – as a cook in the home of a lawyer. Later she had married fellow migrant William Symes, a townsman or carter for the railway, and they had lived in some of Manchester's poorest districts. Elizabeth had given birth to six children of whom four survived to adulthood. Certain details on Elizabeth's funeral bill, however, alerted me to the fact that Elizabeth and her family must have 'gone up' in the world to quite a considerable degree by the time she died. An aunt – who was a young woman at the time of the funeral – confirmed that Elizabeth (her granny) had had 'a really good send off'.

A Quality Affair

According to the funeral bill, my great-grandmother had a 'good quality, polished oak coffin with panelled sides and silver mounts' costing £12. I

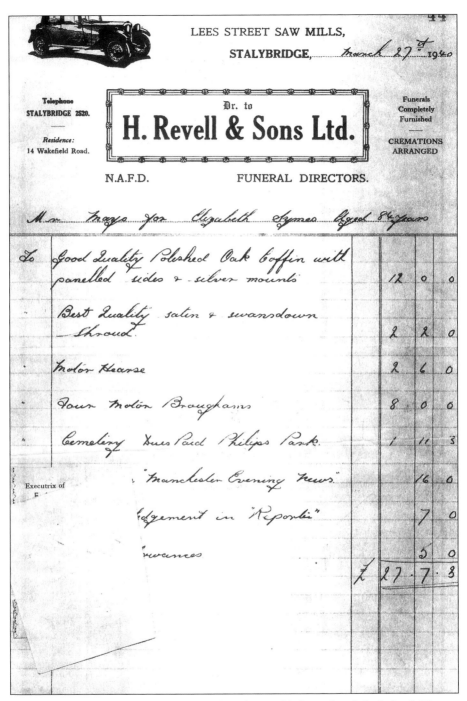

LEES STREET SAW **MILLS**,

STALYBRIDGE, *march 27^d 1940*

Telephone
STALYBRIDGE 2520.

Residence:
14 Wakefield Road.

Dr. to

H. Revell & Sons Ltd.

Funerals
Completely
Furnished

CREMATIONS
ARRANGED

N.A.F.D.   FUNERAL DIRECTORS.

Mr Mayo for Elizabeth Symes Aged 84 years

		£	s	d
To	Good Quality Polished Oak Coffin with panelled sides & silver mounts	12	0	0
"	Best Quality satin & swansdown Shroud	2	2	0
"	Motor Hearse	2	6	0
"	Four Motor Broughams	8	0	0
"	Cemetery Dues Paid Philips Park	1	11	3
	"Manchester Evening News"		16	0
	dgement in "Reporter"		7	0
	wances		5	0
	£	27	7	8

Executrix of
E.

The funeral bill led me on to many other pieces of information. It includes i) The name of the man who paid the bill, my great-uncle Jo Mayo; ii) Reference to Philips Park Cemetery where Elizabeth is buried; iii) Reference to the Acknowledgement of the death in the *Manchester Evening News*; iv) Half-blanked out but still legible: reference to the 'Acknowledgment' of the death in the *Stalybridge Reporter*. (Author's collection)

noticed that it was 'good' quality, not 'best' quality. Nevertheless, the silver mounts must have looked quite impressive. Moreover, no expense was spared on Elizabeth's death dress. She was clothed in a 'best quality satin and swansdown shroud' to the tune of £2 and 20 shillings. In an area of Manchester still known today for its horse-drawn hearses, Elizabeth's motor hearse (costing £2 and 6 shillings) probably caused quite a stir. And behind the coffin came the family – plenty of them by the looks of it – in four motor broughams costing £8. The bill even has a sketch of a brougham in the top left-hand corner, as if to make the point that this was a funeral of some style.

A Lady of Two Obituaries
The funeral bill started me on a fascinating paper chase. It mentioned a death notice in the *Manchester Evening News* which cost 16 shillings, and an 'Acknowledgement' in the local *Stalybridge Reporter* which cost 7 shillings. Unfortunately, the contents of neither of these two papers can yet be viewed at the British Newspaper Archive online (www.british newspaperarchive.co.uk), so I started by visiting the Manchester Archive and Local Studies Centre. As the funeral bill was dated 27 March 1940, I ascertained that Elizabeth must have been buried shortly before that time. After a search of the newspaper microfilms of the *Manchester Evening News* for the week preceding 27 March in Manchester City Library, I found what I had been looking for:

SYMES
On March 22nd, at her daughter's residence, Flaxfield Avenue, Stalybridge, Elizabeth, widow of the late William SYMES, of Manchester, aged 84 years. Service at Wesleyan Chapel, Millbrook, prior to interment at Philips Park Cemetery, Manchester on Wednesday March 27th at 3pm. Reunited. 'Loved by us all'.

The obituary told me something that I didn't know before. Elizabeth's funeral service had been held at a Wesleyan chapel, showing that by the mid-twentieth century at any rate the Symes family were Methodists rather than Anglicans. This was of great interest to me; I had long suspected that the hymn-singing and teetotalism on that side of the family smacked of Methodism, but I hadn't known where to go for further information.

I next contacted the very helpful archivist at Tameside Record Office and suggested a likely range of dates between which the 'Acknowledgement'

Death of Mrs. E. Symes

Funeral at Manchester

The death occurred on Friday, at 19, Flaxfield Avenue, Brushes Estate, Stalybridge, of Mrs. Elizabeth Symes, a native of Manchester, who came to live with her daughter about eight years ago. She was 84 years of age, and whilst she had been at Stalybridge she had identified herself with the Wesley Methodist Church, Millbrook, where she will be much missed.

The interment was at St. Philip's Cemetery, Manchester, on Wednesday. preceded by service at Millbrook Chapel conducted by the Rev. S. Ogden Schofield, resident minister. A tribute to her work was paid by Mr. T. W. Boon, who also offered prayer at her home. Mr. Schofield officiated at the graveside. Four of her nephews acted as bearers.

The mourners were: Mr. and Mrs. Mayo, Mrs. Avison and Marjorie, Mr. and Mrs. Winstanley and Elsie, Mr. and Mrs. Symes and Billie, Mr. and Mrs. G. Webster (Thorne), Mr. Jim Terrell (Mellor), Mr. and Mrs. Joseph Terrell (Manchester), Miss Lilian Terrell (Pontefract), Mr. Charles Terrell (Manchester), Mr. A. Terrell (Sale Moor), Mr. Dibble (Audenshaw), and Miss M. and L. Hoyle (Longsight).

Floral tributes were from: Emmie and Joe; Phyllis, Charlie and Marjorie; Jimmie; Will and Elsie; Jack, Alice and Billie; sister Annie and family; brother Jim and family; brother Charles and niece Lillie; brother and sister, Joe and Jane and family; Mr. and Mrs. Charles Terrell and family; Mr. and Mrs. A. Terrell; Mr. and Mrs. Dibble; the Misses Hoyle; Mr. and Mrs. Harrison and Betty (York); Mr. and Mrs. Snowden (York); Mr. and Mrs. Gillings (York); Nellie, Lizzie, Deborah and Jim; Mr. and Mrs. Boon; Mr. and Mrs. F. Thornley and family; all at No. 8, Flaxfield-avenue; Mr. and Mrs. H. Thornley and Barbara; Mr. and Mrs. A. G. Thornley and family; Mr. and Mrs. Fitton and Ethel; Mr. and Mrs. T. Bamford; Miss A. Sidebottom and Mrs. Coates; Mr. and Mrs. L. Woolliscroft; Mr. and Mrs. Heywood; Mrs. Bennett and Mr. and Mrs. Wilson; neighbours of Flaxfields-avenue; mothers of Millbrook Wesley Methodist Church; the officials and teachers of Millbrook Wesley Methodist Sunday School; Young Ladies' Class at Millbrook Wesley School; and the church and congregation at the Wesley Hall, Ancoats, Manchester.

Messrs. H. Revell and Sons, Ltd., of 12 and 14, Wakefield-road, had charge of the arrangements.

Acknowledgement/obituary of Elizabeth Symes in the *Stalybridge Reporter*, 29 March 1940.

a) Watch out for factual mistakes. This obituary claims that my great-grandmother was a 'native of Manchester,' when in fact she was born in Henstridge, Somerset, and lived in the South West until she was in her mid-twenties.

b) Look out for the names of institutions (particularly churches and chapels) with which the deceased was connected. They may have records which can give you more clues about your ancestors.

c) A list of those donating flowers can be helpful since it groups together the names of people in distinct branches of the family.

d) Mourners are helpfully listed with the place in which they lived.

e) Details about Elizabeth's early life as a glover and a cook are omitted from the obituary, as are references to her twin daughters who died in infancy.

f) Be wary of typographical mistakes. 'Jimmie' here should be 'Jennie'

(Microfilm of the *Stalybridge Reporter* from Tameside Archive Service, Stockport)

of Elizabeth's death might have appeared in the *Stalybridge Reporter*. Before long, an electronic image of the microfilm arrived in an email. To my delight, it turned out to be a fairly long obituary. This provided me with several pieces of information about my great-grandmother that I hadn't previously known.

According to the wording on the obituary, Elizabeth had not been just an ordinary member of the Methodist Church. She had 'identified herself' with it and would be 'much missed' by the congregation. Elizabeth had evidently been an active chapel member because – as I also learned from the obituary – a special tribute had been paid to her 'work' at the funeral. Moreover, there was also mention of 'the church and congregation at the Wesley Hall, Ancoats, Manchester', near to where Elizabeth had lived earlier in her life. From just a couple of column inches then, I had two new sources of enquiry. And I still had the added bonus of reading through the names and addresses of family mourners and those donating floral tributes – a list which enabled me to fill in many missing pieces in the family tree.

Grave and Burial Plot Certificates

A later search among family papers revealed another interesting document – a bill for the plot and gravestone of Elizabeth's husband, William. He died a third of a century before her from pulmonary tuberculosis on 25 February 1907 at the age of 51 years and was buried in Phillip's Park Cemetery. Elizabeth paid a modest £1 and 1 shilling for the grave space and a further 13 shillings for the excavation.

When William died, his daughters were in their teens and would probably have been earning very little. His son was still a boy and Elizabeth no longer worked in any formal sense. I expect that William's funeral would have reflected the family's poverty and that there would have been no silver-mounted coffin for him. The grave was a 'flat grave' and there is no mention of a fee for an inscription. This indicates that – at that time – the Symes family were not wealthy enough to pay for an upright headstone.

In the same year that her husband died (1907), Elizabeth purchased a certificate (also thankfully preserved among the family papers), granting her 'the exclusive right of burial, in perpetuity, in the grave number 319, Section I', for the sum of one pound and one shilling. It was to be 33 years before she joined her husband in that grave.

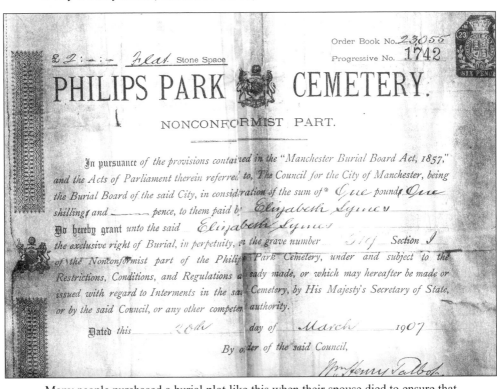

Grave certificate: details of the burial of Elizabeth's husband William in 1907 suggest a very ordinary affair. (Author's collection)

Many people purchased a burial plot like this when their spouse died to ensure that they would be buried in the same grave. (Author's collection)

With the information I now had, I was able to search for a record of Elizabeth's burial at www.burialrecords.manchester.gov.uk. For a small fee, this service allows you to search for up to four burials in certain Manchester cemeteries. After a simple keyword search, I was presented with the 'Deceased Details' of Elizabeth Symes and discovered that she was indeed buried in grave number 319 of section I of Philips Park Cemetery. As was to be expected, she was buried in the non-conformist part of the cemetery and I guessed she would be with my great-grandfather.

Locating the Grave

My final task was actually to locate the grave of Elizabeth and William Symes. Philips Park is a huge municipal cemetery with sections for Anglican, Nonconformist, Jewish and Roman Catholic graves, reflecting the diversity of Manchester's population since the late nineteenth century. Records of the cemetery since 1866 are held at the Manchester Archives and Local Studies Centre. A quick look at their website (www. manchester.gov.uk/info/448/archives-and-local-history) assured me that my great-grandparents' grave ought still to be intact. Only graves in 'D' section, the site informed me, were exhumed and re-interred in 1992 to make way for an intermediate ring road around the city.

In common with many Victorian cemeteries, Philips Park has separate entrances for Anglican and Nonconformist burials. Once I had discovered this, it was easy enough to find Section 'I' and grave number '319', since each gravestone has a number inscribed into its bottom right-hand corner and the plots are arranged numerically. The grave of my great-grandparents is in a quiet corner bordering a wall beyond which is one of Manchester's busiest thoroughfares. The flat stone commemorating the death of William must have been replaced on Elizabeth's death, for there is now a headstone, small but upright. Touchingly – and emphasising the family's closeness, the language of the inscription mirrors the language of Elizabeth's obituary in the *Manchester Evening News* – 'Loved by us all'.

By putting the different pieces of information together, I could see that by the middle of the twentieth century, the Symes family must have worked their way up from deep poverty to respectability. Elizabeth's three surviving daughters had married well. Their husbands were the owner of a dairy, the manager of a temperance bar (who was also an alderman) and a senior worker in the gasworks. Their brother (my grandfather, William John Symes) was the manager of a Freeman, Hardy and Willis Boot and

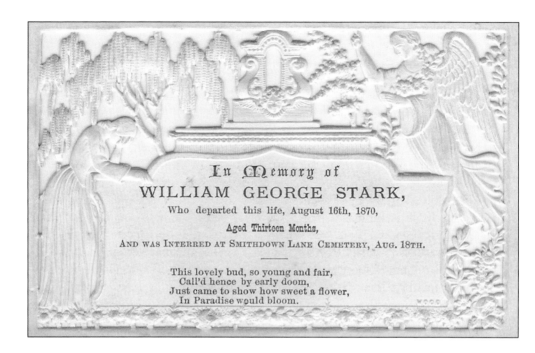

In Memory of
WILLIAM GEORGE STARK,
Who departed this life, August 16th, 1870,

Aged Thirteen Months,

AND WAS INTERRED AT SMITHDOWN LANE CEMETERY, AUG. 18TH.

This lovely bud, so young and fair,
Call'd hence by early doom,
Just came to show how sweet a flower,
In Paradise would bloom.

Victorian mourning cards like these can you give you dates of death, ages, names of cemeteries and dates of burial. (Author's collection)

In Affectionate Remembrance of
John William Jones,
Who was accidentally killed whilst in the execution of his duty, on January 26th, 1885,
Aged 27 Years,
And was interred at Smithdown Road Cemetery, on the 29th Jan.
——:o:——
" Be ye, therefore, ready ; for in such an hour as ye think not,
the Son of Man cometh."
——:o.——
"In the midst of life we are in death."

Shoe Shop. By the end of her life, Elizabeth was living with her eldest daughter, Emmie, in the leafy suburb of Stalybridge, a far cry from the Manchester slums where she had spent her middle years. In 1940, the Symeses were not rich, but they had at least made the ranks of the lower middle-class and were able to pool together their resources to give their mother a decent send off.

As I stood in that Manchester graveyard, I imagined the Symes family in 1940 gathered to see their mother off whilst their motorised broughams waited just beyond the wall. But most of all, I thought of Elizabeth buried under my feet – like a lady – in her polished oak coffin and satin and swansdown shroud and I reflected that it was not such a bad end for a poor glover's daughter.

Key Sources: Records Related to Death (particularly Obituaries)
Records related to the deaths of ancestors can paradoxically tell you a great deal about their lives. Evidence about funerals, for example, can alert you to your ancestor's status in the family and in society, their wealth, their social pretensions and their religious beliefs. Of all the various death-related records, the obituary is probably the most useful. No other source of information can beat a mini-biography of your ancestor finished off, perhaps, with an adroit assessment of his or her character. If you are lucky enough to locate an obituary for a member of your family, make sure that you temper your delight with some caution, however. Obituaries may distort, mislead or misrepresent. Handle obituaries with care and you will be rewarded with an insight not just into your ancestor's life but into the times in which he or she lived.

Where might I find obituaries about my ancestor?
Depending on the kind of person your ancestor was – his or her social status, occupation and interests – an obituary might turn up in one or more of a number of different kinds of publication. National and local newspapers, as we have said, might have been digitised and might be available to view for a small fee at www.britishnewspaperarchive.co.uk. The other types of publication mentioned below might be stored in local or national archives (search for them via www.nationalarchives.gov.uk) or in the archives of the institution to which they are connected.

• national newspapers (if your ancestor was very famous)

- local or regional newspapers (bear in mind that obituaries are more likely to be found in a newspaper local to the place in which a person lived for most of their lives rather than in a paper local to the place in which he or she died)
- church magazines, company or society newsletters
- alumni magazines from colleges and universities
- trade journals
- professional journals.

Bear in mind that obituaries in local papers would probably have appeared two to three days after the death (if they were announcing the funeral) and a week or two weeks after the death (if they were reporting the funeral). It's possible that obituaries in any other publications might have appeared as long as several months after the death. *The British Medical Journal*, for example, records the obituaries of over 400 doctors per year and asks only that obituaries be submitted within three months of a death.

What might I be able to find out about my ancestor from an obituary?
An obituary can be a goldmine for the family historian. For ordinary people, local newspaper obituaries are likely to carry longer obituaries than city newspapers. Obituaries in journals again will be longer and fuller. Information can include some or all of the following details:

- name
- occupation
- date and cause of death
- circumstances of death
- birth date
- birthplace
- list of surviving relatives
- mention of close relatives (such as a spouse) who have recently died
- marriage information
- membership of organisations
- military service
- education
- employment history
- outstanding achievements
- offices held

- hobbies and activities
- funeral, memorial and burial arrangements
- names of pallbearers
- names of mourners
- names of those who donated flowers.

All of these items, of course, may provide the starting-point for further investigation of certificates, graveyards and cemeteries, military and employment records. By naming offspring and other mourners, obituaries also greatly aid the search for surviving relatives.

Think laterally
Look out for bias. Don't forget that relatives probably paid a fee per line or per word for the obituary – this will have had an effect on what they chose to include. Ask yourself who wrote the obituary (a relative, a friend, a colleague, an employer, a newspaper reporter, the funeral director)? Ask yourself where the writer obtained his/her information and whether or not it is likely to have been accurate?

Consider the kind of publication in which the obituary appears – a left-wing trade union journal will probably report your ancestor's life quite differently from a church magazine, for example.

Be aware that errors and inaccuracies do occur. Look out for large gaps in the chronology of your ancestor's life that are unaccounted for and for omissions (a first marriage or a period in prison may not be mentioned, for example).

Beware of euphemisms that may have been used to cover up something unpleasant like a bankruptcy or a spell in prison. Look out for clichés: statements such as 'Adored by all his colleagues' or 'We shall not see his like again' may be the result of a lack of imagination on the part of the writer rather than any genuine exceptional qualities on the part of your ancestor.

Resources to Take You Further
Books
Baranick, Alana, Sheeler, Jim and Miller, Stephen, *Life on the Death Beat: A Handbook for Obituary Writers*, Marion Street Press, 2005.
Brooks, C., *Mortal Remains: The History and Present State of the Victorian Cemetery*, Wheaton, 1989.
Brunskill, Ian (ed.), *Great Lives: A Century in Obituaries*, Times Books, 2006.

Heritage, Celia, *Tracing Your Ancestors Through Death Records: A Guide For Family Historians*, Pen and Sword Books, 2013.

Jalland, Pat, *Death in the Victorian Family*, OUP, 1996.

Litten. Julian, *The English Way of Death*, Robert Hale, 2002.

May, Trevor, *Victorian Undertaker*, Shire, 1996.

Starck, Nigel, *Life after Death: A Celebration of the Obituary Art*, Melbourne University Press, 2006.

Wright, G., *Discovering Epitaphs*, Shire, 2003.

Websites

www.burial-inscriptions.co.uk – a photographic record of UK churches, churchyards, graveyards and cemeteries.

www.burialrecords.manchester.gov.uk Search here for ancestors buried in Manchester cemeteries.

www.cemeteryfriends.org.uk/National Federation of Cemetery Friends. Groups of volunteers interested in conserving cemeteries large and small.

www.culture24.org.uk/am24234 Manchester Archives and Local Studies Centre.

www.deceasedonline.com Central database for UK burials and cremations including photographs of graves and memorials, cemetery maps, and details of other occupants in the same grave.

www.freepages.genealogy.rootsweb.com/obitl List of Obituary Look Up Volunteers who will search for your ancestor's obituary in local papers on your behalf.

www.gravematters.org.uk On how to transcribe memorial inscriptions.

www.gravestonephotos.com/ A photographic record of many gravestones around the country.

www.historyfromheadstones.com Large collection of graveyard inscriptions from Northern Ireland. Full access requires subscription.

www.interment.net/uk/index.htm UK cemetery records.

www.vam.ac.uk/content/galleries/level-4/room-125b-birth-marriage-and-death/ The Victoria and Albert Museum's collection on Victorian birth, marriage and death.

Addresses
The Victoria and Albert Museum
Cromwell Road
London SW7 2RL

CHAPTER 7

'We Come Alive Behind Shop Counters'

Focus on History: Working for Big Companies
Key Source: Company Newsletters and Company Archives

High-street retailers such as Marks and Spencer, Boots and John Lewis have employed many thousands of our ancestors since the late nineteenth century. Companies and families were often intimately entwined. Some employees will have joined as youngsters and may have met their future spouses at work. In some families, son followed father and daughter followed mother into employment with the same company. For those who stayed a good number of years (sometimes up to sixty), the company may have marked their retirement in some way. In addition to this, several big companies styled themselves as 'extended families' and expected employees to share values and a code of conduct. Because of all these

Career girls: from left to right, Phyllis, Emmie and Jenny Symes, c. 1906. The back of this photograph indicates that it was taken in Hull – the town to which the girls moved to work for Marks and Spencer. (Author's collection)

factors, if you seek to find out more about a particular company, you also stand to learn a great deal about the lives of your ancestors.

The Story

There has long been a saying in my family that we 'come alive behind shop counters'. Give us a set of shelves and a till and we will become at once energised and happy. Inherited bits of wisdom like this – suggesting that particular acumen or talents have been passed down through the family – are worth investigating. It's true that there are plenty of shopkeepers and small businessmen in the family now, but the saying itself, I believe, originates from much further back. My suspicions were confirmed when I found among the family papers, a company newsletter from Marks and Spencer (*St Michael News*) from 1959. I immediately noticed that the front cover showed a photograph of my great-aunt Emmie Mayo (née Symes) as an elderly lady.

The article is a special feature for Christmas and describes what the festive season would have been like at Marks and Spencer fifty years previously. At 72, Emmie was probably one of the store's oldest ex-employees; and her memories must have been considered a fascinating source of seasonal copy by the writers on the magazine. In the article, Emmie recalls how she initially worked as a Saturday girl in the Oldham Street Store in Manchester more than half a century previously. There is also a footnote – which was invaluable to me – which records that Emmie's sisters, Phyllis and Jenny, also worked in the same Manchester store. In the second column of the article, there are a couple of delightful reminiscences from Emmie as she describes how her father had once been unhappy about the fact that her employers had asked her to 'put her hair up', and how Mr Marks used to give the girls buttered teacakes and coffee on New Year's Eve.

Evidently, Emmie and her sisters (who were born in the late 1880s and early 1890s), were some of the earliest employees of Marks and Spencer. This knowledge fitted with the fact that they had been born in very part of North Manchester where the company had started. Inspired by the newsletter, I read a company history written to celebrate its centenary (Asa Briggs, *Marks and Spencers 1884-1984 – A Centenary History* (1984)) which described how in 1893, Mr Michael Marks, a Russian-born Polish refugee, first moved to 20 Cheetham Hill Road, Manchester. Marks's early career had been as a trader at Kirkgate Market in Leeds.

St Michael NEWS

MARKS & SPENCER LTD.
VOL 6 No 12   DECEMBER 1959

Our warm good wishes

I am happy to have the opportunity of sending you my personal greetings from our new Head Offices in Baker Street.

Many of you are witnessing a transformation of the stores in which you are working. I know you share my pride in these beautiful stores, which not only enable us to display attractively the expanding range of ST. MICHAEL goods but also make shopping a pleasure for our customers. As you are aware the Board is equally concerned with your own comfort and well-being. It is with this in mind that we design the pleasant staff quarters which we hope you enjoy.

During the past months we have invited many distinguished citizens to look behind the scenes in your local stores. You will have heard their complimentary remarks on the conditions and amenities we provide for the staff and they particularly welcome our campaign for clean stores and clean foods in which you play a vital part.

We have since received hundreds of letters from them, and articles from the local Press, telling us how much they appreciate our efforts.

To the newcomers among our staff I take this opportunity to extend a welcome - they are joining colleagues whose courtesy and friendly service have won the high regard of the Board and of our ever-increasing numbers of customers.

Also, to our growing numbers of pensioners, I would like to send a special greeting, for we feel, as I hope they do, that they are still members of the Marks and Spencer family.

This year all our manufacturers and their staffs are reading ST. MICHAEL NEWS for the first time, which enables me to offer my greetings to them personally. It is with their help and co-operation that we achieve the quality and value which the public associates with our brand name, ST. MICHAEL.

To all who share in Marks and Spencer's endeavour to serve the public, I send on behalf of the Board our warm good wishes for Christmas and the New Year.

Simon Marks

NO SMOKING PLEASES

CUSTOMER AND PRESS COMMENT

THERE has been press comment on the company's "No Smoking" campaign, as well as a generally favourable public reaction.

Says *The Guardian*: "Quietly and without any advance publicity, Marks & Spencer have decided to stop customers smoking in all their 237 branches in Britain."

The *Daily Sketch* quoted Sir Simon Marks: "It takes courage to be pioneers, and we have it.

"People thought customers would be frightened away when members of our staff started telling them to stub their cigarettes out.

"Instead, customers said they were delighted to shop in a smoke-free store."

A silent revolution

Said *The Star*: "There's been a silent revolution in the shopping world. Marks & Spencer have banned smoking in their 237 stores. It is one of the boldest moves in the retail trade for years."

The ban was recorded in *The Times*, in *Reynolds News* and the *Evening Standard*.

In the *Bucks Free Press* Mr. R. F. Shapter, Chief Public Health Inspector for High Wycombe commented: "I think it is a good example which other shops might well follow: Hygiene apart I do not think it fair for shop assistants to have to work in a smokey atmosphere".

The operation of the ban has not been without its humorous side.

At Brixton a customer who had been asked to put his cigarette out, agreed.

A few minutes later the manager was astounded to see this same customer asking another customer to put *his* cigarette out.

A number of complimentary letters have also been received.

Party timely

THREE or four dozen lucky stores have just received first deliveries of party skirts at a gift-happy price of 42s. 6d. One style is in an exciting new fabric—rayon/boucle and some of the colours have that fashionable "metallised" finish. There's also a style that's rayon/boucle one side, taffeta the other. A third is all-taffeta reversing from black to bright colour. They'd be delighted to team up with your party tops.

Here's Humph!

Humphrey Lyttelton and his band are to play at the Administration Group's party at Hannah House later in the month.

★ Mrs. Mayo—she used to be Emmy Symes when she managed Hull— with a plate that cost her a penny.

Christmas 50 years ago — she kept the takings in her muff

St. Michael News Reporter

WHEN, just after midnight on Christmas Eve, the last M & S customer had left Hepworth's Arcade in Hull, the manageress used to take home such cash as she'd been unable to bank in a box. It was nearly all gold, the pubs had taken most of the silver, and the copper she used to hide in the shop. The year was 1909.

Nervous but conscientious, she watched that money like a hen with her chicks. If she went out of the house the money went with her.

Indeed, one of the most vivid memories of Emmy Symes*, for that was her name then, is sitting in church with the day's takings clutched tightly in her muff.

Her two sisters worked with her on Saturday afternoons at Oldham Street, later accompanied her to Hull.

Today Emmy Symes is Mrs. Mayo of Stalybridge, Cheshire, and retired of course, but her memories stay fresh.

Her hair up

This was Christmas at Marks & Spencer fifty years ago:

It was the present Mr. Jacobson's father telling her to put her hair up if she wanted to get on, and her father refusing at first but finally yielding. It was Mr. Marks giving the girls buttered tea cakes and coffee on Christmas Eve.

It was selling a toy engine to a little boy who one day became the chairman of Marks & Spencer. It was a week's wages and an umbrella, for a Christmas present. It was walking to Robert Street Cheetham with the week's orders and joking with Mr. Norris' father. It was pretending not to hear when visiting football fans likened their blue overalls and red ties to a then popular club.

It was selling lines like mince pie cutters in three different sizes, 12-hole patty tins, and nut crackers—all for a penny of course.

Rubber heels

It was selling, for the same price: cigars, pairs of rubber heels complete with screws, coal rakes, egg cups, tambourines, potato mashers, mouth organs, books of carols, serviettes (two dozen), crackers (three in a box), glass balls and glass animals, paper hats, small saucepans, large loo-fahs, skipping ropes, flags—the list is fantastic in its range.

Mrs. Mayo remembers them all, remembers selling them too, and it should please the Mrs. Mayos of the company to know that from time to time, fifty and more years later, this old merchandise keeps cropping up, often still doing yeoman service.

A combined needle box and pin cushion, for instance, with a mirror inside the lid which cost a penny from the first week's wages of a 14-year-old seamstress named Elsie, at M & S Harrow Road.

Or a set of patterned tea spoons, like these belonging to Mrs. E. B. Harris of Worthing. Her mother-in-law bought them 57 years ago at Guildford Penny Bazaar.

★ Mrs. Harris's spoons

His patron saint . . . ?

THIS is the story of how little Tony Rapley of Eltham learnt about St. Michael and Marks & Spencer.

A few weeks ago, Tony's parents wrote to Sir Simon Marks:

"As well as being a Prince* and a Sir, in our son's estimation you are also a saint.

"When told we couldn't afford a car to take him around in, he is a polio victim, he said: 'never mind Mummy, I'll pray to St. Michael for one, he gives us a lot of other things'."

This letter did not go unnoticed. A large Meccano set "From St. Michael" was sent off, and earned this reply:

"Dear St. Michael,

"Thank you for the Meccano set which you sent me. In the school holidays I am going to make a single-deck bus. Mummy tells me you work for Marks & Spencer.

Love from
Tony Rapley."

Sir Simon was called "The Prince of Chain Stores" in a recent "Star" article.

THIS WAS TOOTING 50 YEARS AGO

★ And this was how Tooting must have looked at Christmas 1909. It was sent in by a Mr. Smith of Gloucester Street, Brighton—that's his wife, third from the right. "It certainly shows the progress made by Marks & Spencers in 50 years," comments Mr. Smith. It does indeed . . . why even the managers (far left) don't dress like that any more.

Page One

After this, he had opened many market stalls across the North of England. In 1894, a year after he moved to Manchester, Marks opened a shop in the lower part of his home and, in the same year, he formed a partnership with Tom Spencer, a former cashier from the wholesale company I.J. Dewhirst. Thus began the retail chain Marks and Spencer.

Whilst these momentous historical events were occurring, my great aunts Emmie, Phyllis and Jenny Symes were growing up nearby with their parents William and Elizabeth and their younger brother William John (Jack) – the little boy who would become my grandfather. Two other sisters (twins) had already died. The children grew up in Ancoats and Bradford – two of the poorest parts of Manchester.

Found among family papers, a photo of Tom Spencer. (Author's collection)

So in this story, there is a contrast that makes for drama: on the one hand, the enterprising commercial partnership poised to take over the country, on the other – and in close geographical proximity – an obscure working-class family struggling to make ends meet. How the two came together is a matter for speculation but here another piece of family folklore proved useful. Several relatives had muttered to me that my great-grandfather William Symes knew Mr Marks and Mr Spencer personally. This seems plausible. As a railway townsman (or carter) in the last decade of the nineteenth century, William would have carried goods by horse and cart from Manchester's Victoria Station to local businesses including the new Marks and Spencer stores in Cheetham Hill and Oldham Street.

A friendship between Mr Symes, Mr Marks and Mr Spencer was apparently struck and, with his familiar knowledge of the ins-and-outs of Manchester's streets and alleyways, William was able, it has been rumoured, to suggest to his new friends a potential location for new business premises in the city. Whilst I will never know whether or not this story is true, it is backed up to some extent by the published company history. Certainly, the entrepreneurial duo were looking for somewhere to house their new warehouse and head office in 1901, and soon settled on a location in Robert Street, Strangeways, very close to where the Symes family lived.

One of the earliest Marks and Spencer branches at 60 Oldham Street, Manchester, 1898. The Symes sisters worked here. (By permission of Marks and Spencer plc)

Jobs for the Girls

In the 1901 census, the Symes family, by now residing in Bradford, Manchester, were living in pretty desperate circumstances. Apart from father William, eldest daughter Emmie was the only member of the family who worked. At 14, she is recorded on the census as a 'shop assistant (draper)': whether or not this was for Marks and Spencer isn't clear. However, according to the Marks and Spencer archive, the retail chain had opened no fewer than five outlets in the Manchester area by 1902 and it is likely that at this point William called in a favour from his successful friends and found work first for Emmie and then for Phyllis and Jenny in the nearest Marks and Spencer's shop in Oldham Street (which opened on 28 March 1898).

I wanted to know more about what working conditions were like for the Symes sisters. Unfortunately, the company archive doesn't keep detailed information on individual employees, but there is plenty of general material including many photographs of the early stores. There were two different kinds of Marks and Spencer's shop in the early days: the stores themselves and the Penny Bazaars. The Bazaars had no doors and employees often complained of the cold. Being a benevolent employer, Mr Marks had special wooden pallets installed to help keep the girls' feet off the ground. There was a gangway six or seven feet wide for customers and the goods would be on open display on a horseshoe-shaped counter.

In the company magazine, Emmie recalled that in the early days, she had sold 'mince pie cutters in three different sizes, 12 hole patty tins, nut crackers, cigars, pairs of rubber heels, coal rakes, egg cups, tambourines, potato mashers, mouth organs, books of carols, 2 dozen serviettes, 3

'Value, Variety, Quality and Quantity'. Marks and Spencer's Store, Oldham Street, Manchester, 1925. (By permission of Marks and Spencer plc)

crackers in a box, glass balls and glass animals, paper hats, small saucepans, large loofahs, skipping ropes and flags'. Everything cost a penny and trade thrived on the fact that everything could be seen and handled. This was a new idea in shops, although it had of course been practised for centuries on markets. Another attractive feature of the Marks and Spencer stores and bazaars was the fact that there was no haggling about price – something quite unlike market trading. For the staff – including presumably my great aunts – there were long hours. Marks and Spencer stores were open six days a week with one day only being an early closing day. On market days, they were always very busy.

Deaths of Messrs Marks, Spencer and Symes

In the early years of the twentieth century, the world around the Symes girls was changing fast. Within the space of two and a half years (between July 1905 and December 1907), not only Mr Marks and Mr Spencer but also their own father was dead. William Symes passed away on 25 February 1907 at the age of 51 years from pulmonary tuberculosis. At his death, Emmie, Phyllis and Jenny were just 19, 18 and 16 years old. It must have been a desperate time for them particularly as they had their younger brother Jack, aged 12, as well as their mother to support.

It was during this difficult time – probably in 1906 as their father was ailing – that Marks and Spencer really came to the rescue, almost as an extended family might have done. By 1906, the company had forty-nine stores and an annual turnover of £151,000. In her interview in *St Michael News*, Emmie revealed that when Marks and Spencer opened their store in Hepworth's Arcade, Hull, she took up a position there as manageress. The helpful footnote records that her sisters soon followed her there. The geographical move combined with the levels of responsibility must have been quite a challenge for three fatherless young women in the first decade of the twentieth century.

A member of the family told me that Emmie Symes stayed in Hull until she returned to Manchester to marry. Jenny also became a Marks and Spencer manageress in Hull until she too went back to marry her fiancé in Manchester. Phyllis went to work for the 'Pavement' branch of Marks and Spencer in York and, after a brief stint at the Birmingham branch of the store, returned to that city to marry.

The company newsletter with its interview with Emmie, brought alive some of the detail of life as a Marks and Spencer's manageress in the

'Don't Ask the Price It's a Penny'. Marks and Spencer, Hepworth's Arcade, Hull, branch where Emmie was manageress in the first decade of the twentieth century. (By permission of Marks and Spencer plc)

early years of the twentieth century. In it, Emmie recalls being in charge of the takings. On Christmas Eve, 1909, she was faced with a dilemma – she had to take care of the money taken that week but was unable to bank it straight away. With characteristic resourcefulness, she exchanged as many small coins for gold coins as she could with local businesses and then put these in a box and took them to church with her on Christmas morning hidden for safekeeping in her muff! The published history of Marks and Spencer tells me that the average annual turnover per Marks and Spencer store in 1909 was £3,500. From this, I can work out the weekly turnover of an average store. Together with a little extra factored in for Christmas, it would seem that Emmie probably had quite a substantial amount of money in that muff!

By the time they married (before and shortly after the First World War) the Symes sisters had come a long way. If the family saying that they 'came alive behind shop counters' is anything to go by, they loved their work and were good at it. Certainly, they were well able to support their mother and brother from afar until Jack, my grandfather, was old enough to work himself. As an old man, he remembered the efforts of his trio of working elder sisters with respect. Their long years of dedication to a well-established company had helped to lift the family from potential destitution into the ranks of the lower-middle class.

Emmie Symes holding the photograph of her one-time employer, Tom Spencer. The pose suggests that she knew him personally. (Author's collection)

Key Source: Company Newsletters and Company Archives

Your ancestor may have spent most of his/her life working for a single company. If that is the case, then it is likely that there are many clues to this in your family home. Clocks, watches, paintings or pieces of furniture presented on retirement and adorned with inscriptions or plaques stating the number of years' service can be good starting points for research. You may also find caps and badges with company details, as well as wage slips, passes or pension documents. In addition, in-house journals, company magazines and staff newsletters found among family papers might contain specific references to your ancestors particularly around the time of their retirement or their deaths.

Where can I find out more information about companies for which my ancestors worked?
Some companies have produced one or more published histories (Marks and Spencer is a case in point, see the Books section below). Other companies have in-house archives and archivists willing and able to answer your questions as long as you can provide the names and possible dates of employment of your ancestors (see a selective list of company archive addresses below)

Company archives may hold a wide range of material including

• personnel records
• merchandise

- advertising
- annual reports
- audio-visual sources
- photographs
- board minutes
- accounts
- company newsletters.

What information might I find out about my ancestors from company records?
You are unlikely to find out specific details of the working lives of individuals. But a combination of dedicated books, company websites, and company archives may enable you to find out information on the following:

- what your ancestors were paid
- their probable working hours, conditions and holiday entitlements
- their level of training and responsibility
- whether or not they received sickness benefits or pensions
- at what age they might have been likely to retire.

The Beacon, March 1923. The Boots magazine for non-retail staff. (By permission of the Boots Archive)

Think laterally
You can find out a lot about your family's overall sense of financial security and welfare in the past by learning about the company for which they worked. Benevolent employers might have helped individuals out in times of hardship. In some manufacturing companies, such as Rowntree's, York, workers were entitled to far more than their wages, enjoying, for example, the benefits of good housing in a special company village, New Earswick, and leisure facilities. Similar benefits were provided by Cadbury's at Bourneville in Birmingham and Lever Brothers at Port Sunlight on the Wirral.

Company history is particularly helpful if you are trying to find out more about the women in your family. Shop work was an increasingly acceptable career for a respectable working-class girl from the late nineteenth century onwards and, during wartime in particular, many women were taken on by big employers to fill the roles vacated by men.

It's worth remembering that women who worked in shops were probably experiencing a kind of financial independence that had been completely beyond the experience of their mothers. Bear in mind too that retirement upon marriage was common for women certainly up to the 1950s.

Resources to Take You Further
Books

Adburgham, Alison, *Shops and Shopping, 1800-1914*, Allen and Unwin, 1964.

Baren, Maurice E, *Victorian Shopping: How it All Began*, Michael O'Mara, 1998.

Bevan, Judi, *The Rise and Fall of Marks and Spencer*, Profile Books. 2001.

Bookbinder, Paul, *Marks and Spencer: The War Years, 1939-1945*, Century Benham, 1989.

Briggs, Asa, *Marks and Spencer: 1884-1984: A Centenary History of Marks and Spencer: The Originators of Penny Bazaars*, Octopus Books, 1984.

Chislett, Helen, *Marks in Time: 125 Years of Marks and Spencer*, W & N, 2009.

Clarke, Eric, *The Story of Sainsbury's*, Hutchinson, 1999.

Davis, Dorothy, *A History of Shopping*, Routledge, 2010.

Hoffman, P.C, *They Also Serve: The Story of the Shopworker*, Porcupine Press, 1949.

Kennedy, Carol, *Business Pioneers: Sainsbury, John Lewis, Cadbury*, Random House Business Books, 2001.

Marchant, Brian, *Boots the Chemist of Nottingham on Old Picture Postcards, Yesterday's Nottinghamshire*, Reflections of a Byegone Age, 1999.

McGregor, Alexandrina, *A Chapbook of Memories of Marks and Spencer: From 1946 to 1980*, East Wittering, 1994.

Paquet, Laura, *The Urge to Splurge: A Social History of Shopping*, E.C.W. Press, 2004.

Steele, Jess, *Rations and Rubble – Remembering Woolworths*, Deptford Forum Publishing, 1994.

Whitaker, Wilfred, *Victorian and Edwardian Shopworkers: The Struggle to Obtain Better Working Conditions and a Half Holiday*, David and Charles, 1973.

Websites

www.archive.museumoflondon.org.uk/SainsburyArchive/ Sainsbury's Archive.www.corporate.marksandspencer.com/aboutus/our-heritage The history of Marks and Spencer from 1864.

www.johnlewismemorystore.org.uk/category/heritage_centre The John Lewis Memory Store.

marksintime.marksandspencer.com/home Marks and Spencer Archive.

www.rowntreesociety.org.uk/rowntree-history-2/ The History of Rowntree of York from 1725.

www.sainsburyslivingarchive.co.uk/ Sainsbury's Living Archive which takes a look at the company's products and selling through time.

www.whsmithplc.co.uk/about_whsmith/history_of_whsmith/ History of WHSmith from 1792.

www.woolworthsmuseum.co.uk/ The complete history of Woolworth's in America and the UK.

Addresses

Boots Archive
Boots plc
D122 Records Centre
Nottingham
England
NG90 4XY

John Lewis Partnership Heritage Centre
Grove Farm
Odney Lane
Cookham
England
SL6 9SR

Marks and Spencer Company Archive
Michael Marks Building
University of Leeds
LS2 9JT

Nestle Rowntree's Archive
The Borthwick Institute

University of York
Heslington
York
YO10 5DD

The Sainsbury's Archive
Museum in Docklands
No 1 Warehouse
West India Quay
London
E14 4AL

WHSmith Archive
University of Reading
Whiteknights
PO Box 217
Reading
Berkshire
RG6 6AH

CHAPTER 8

'Great-Grandfather Lived with the Red Indians'

Focus on History: Emigration to America
Key Source: Passenger Lists

Many of our ancestors emigrated during the nineteenth and early twentieth centuries – to America, to Canada, to Australia and to New Zealand. Others went overseas for short periods of time to work. Finding the list which records the actual passage of your ancestor overseas can be thrilling and can help you to find out far more about him or her than the bare facts of the voyage. Some passenger lists, for instance, will give details of your ancestor's physical appearance and the names and addresses of his or her nearest relatives in the Old World and the New. A lot of other personal detail may also be available. There may be many different reasons why your ancestor felt the need to leave Britain either permanently or temporarily. Simple wanderlust – however appealing an idea to the family historian – is usually not the case. It's far more likely that he or she will have moved for pressing economic, social or religious reasons. Whatever the explanation, passenger lists are important in that they mark a transition from one setting to another in your ancestors' lives and certainly indicate the start of a new chapter in their story.

The Story
Rumours have always abounded about my great-grandfather George Wilkinson (1866–1937) and the time he spent living among the 'Red Indians'. Tomahawks and tepees had always seemed to me to be highly unlikely features of the life of a poor Lancashire miner. In family history, however – to borrow an apt phrase – there is rarely smoke without fire. Portrayed as a loner, and a maverick who travelled to America in the early

This photograph of a group of men in Roslyn, Washington State, in 1890 shows that Native Americans were certainly very much part of the community. (Courtesy of the Local History Collection, Ellensburg Public Library, Ellensburg, Washington, USA)

years of the twentieth century, George's adventures have been seen in the family as not so much courageous as selfish. George, it has been said, went West on a whim to pan for gold and gave no indication of when he was coming back. He finally returned to Wigan some years later penniless and looking like a tramp – or so the story goes.

A Transatlantic Trip

At the very least, I thought, I should find out whether or not George Wilkinson actually made any trip across the Atlantic at all. To resolve the issue, I set about investigating the online passenger lists available at www.ellisislandrecords.org and www.ancestry.co.uk. Since my maternal grandfather (George's son) had complained that his father had deserted the family when he was a young child, I searched for men named George Wilkinson sailing from Liverpool to New York in the five years after my grandfather's birth in 1904. To my delight, I quite quickly discovered a George Wilkinson who travelled to America aboard a ship called the *Lucania* in January 1909. His given address in Argyle Street, Hindley, confirmed that he was the right one.

Transatlantic passenger lists are fascinating genealogical resources. At the turn of the nineteenth and twentieth centuries, more and more information was being required of passengers year by year. As I ran my eyes across the various columns of the *Lucania*'s passenger list, a picture of the character George Wilkinson started to emerge. He declared himself as married and 40 years old (this must have been a white lie – he was actually 42), and a collier. The name and address of his wife Mary is recorded, as is his place of birth, Hindley, near Wigan. For the first time, I could say with reasonable certainty that my great-grandfather was a literate man as there is a tick in the box denoting whether or not he was able to read and write.

By 1909, the amount of detail required on transatlantic passenger lists meant that the entries for each passenger covered two pages. I was delighted to see a lot of detail about George on the second page, albeit of a rather assorted nature. I discovered that he was five foot seven with a pale complexion, brown hair and blue eyes. Fascinatingly, he had a jaw that was crooked on the 'left side'. As I have no photograph of George, this is the best description of him that I am ever likely to get. From subsequent columns on the list, I learned, also that he had never been in a prison, almshouse or institution for care and treatment of the insane,

Passenger list relating to George and Joseph Wilkinson's trip to America in 1909 (they are passengers 24 and 25 on this list). By this time, the amount of information required of passengers travelling to the United States was considerable. (www.ancestry.co.uk)

and had never been supported by charity. He was not a polygamist or an anarchist! His physical and mental health were 'good' and he had no physical or mental deformity.

A Ticket Paid

Passengers to America rarely declared the whole amount of money that they had on them. Often, they had sewn their entire life's savings into the linings of their coats and the hems of their skirts. The passenger list on which George appears in 1909 tells me that he had paid for his voyage – despite family claims that he worked his passage – and that he declared additional funds of only $25 (rather than the expected $50).

The most important piece of information in the passenger list, from my point of view, was the record of George's final destination – a detail written so quickly by the shipping official and yet carrying such import for me – 'Wash. Roslyn'. A quick internet search for 'Roslyn' (at www.en.wikipedia.org/wiki/Roslyn,Washington) revealed it be a remote mining town in Washington State on the eastern edge of the Cascade Mountains. The passenger list states that George was in possession of a single ticket to Roslyn and was not travelling 'as a result of any offer, solicitation, promise or agreement, express or implied to labour in the United States'.

One of Many

George was one of more than 20 million immigrants who arrived in the United States between 1880 and 1920 (the period before the Johnson-Reed Act of 1924 limited the number of immigrants allowed into the country).

The *Lucania*

The Ellis Island website www.ellisisland.com told me a bit more about the ship on which George travelled. Built in Glasgow in 1893, the *Lucania*'s service speed was 21 knots and when George sailed, she reached New York in eight days. Between 1893 and 1897, the *Lucania* was the fastest liner afloat. She could carry 2,000 passengers of whom 600 would have been First Class, 400 Second Class and 1,000 (like George) Third Class. In 1901, she was the first ship in the Cunarder

---

line to have a Marconi Wireless and the first to publish a daily bulletin board based on news obtained through the wireless (1903). George may well have been on the *Lucania*'s last eastbound trip. In August 1909, she burned out and sank in the docks in Liverpool.

George was what is known as a 'bird of passage'. He may not have had a firm offer of work in America, but he most certainly expected to get it. Roslyn was a coalmining town founded in 1886 by the Northern Pacific Company (a subsidiary of the Northern Pacific Railroad) to support the building of the American railroad. The mining provided coal for engines fuelling up for the trip across the Cascade Mountains. After a strike by white American miners in 1888, the Roslyn mines recruited black miners from the east to replace them, and in the early twentieth century, miners from all over Europe came to work in Roslyn. Immigrants like George were a crucial part of the US economy.

Myths Overturned

Whilst I was delighted to find out that part of the legend about George Wilkinson was true, I realised that family gossip has also probably done my great-grandfather a huge disservice. He was no lone and maverick adventurer, but more likely a brave and hardworking breadwinner. In fact, a closer look at the 1909 passenger lists proves that George's passage to America was very much a family – and even a community – affair. The name next to George's on the list is that of his younger brother, Joseph. The two, it states, were on their way to meet their (much older) brother, Rueben, who was already working as a miner in the Roslyn Works.

I searched the online passenger lists further and found Rueben Wilkinson's arrival in America two years earlier in 1907. He was indeed, at that point, en route for Roslyn. Moreover, on that occasion, this elder Wilkinson brother was apparently accompanied by his son, Benjamin, his daughter-in-law and two grandchildren. A quick look at the addresses and final destinations of other passengers on the same page of the 1907 passenger list revealed a large number of men of working age from Lancashire (specifically Westhoughton, Wigan and Leigh) all bound to join relatives or friends in Roslyn. Far from being a man on a lonely mission then, George was in fact one of hundreds of émigré miners from the Lancashire pits who ended up in this small American town. This

After the Explosion of the N.W.I.Co. Shaft At Roslyn, Wash. (Connell, Photo)

This mine explosion in Roslyn on 3 October 1909 took place just nine months after George Wilkinson's arrival. (Courtesy of the Local History Collection, Ellensburg Public Library, Ellensburg, Washington, USA)

A group of miners in Roslyn in 1917. (Courtesy of the Local History Collection, Ellensburg Public Library, Ellensburg, Washington, USA)

discovery prompted me to contact the archivist at Wigan Archives Service (at www.wlct.org/Culture/Heritage/archives.htm) who informed me that the skills of miners such as George were so highly regarded at the turn of the century, that they were sometimes granted free passage to America.

The Roslyn Miner
Using websites, and a book dedicated to the history of the area that I discovered on the internet (Shideler, John C., *Coal Towns in the Cascades: A Centennial History of Roslyn and Cle Elum, Washington*, Melior Publications, 1986), I managed to piece together what life might have been like for George amidst the snow and pinewoods of a small town in rural America. The influx of foreign miners swelled Roslyn's small population so that by the 1920s there were about 4,000 inhabitants (four times, incidentally, the number that live there today). The town was also richly multi-ethnic with – eventually – twenty-five separate but adjacent cemeteries to accommodate the dead from all the different cultural groups.

This shot of snow-covered Roslyn in 1920 shows the remoteness of its location. How different from English mining towns such as Wigan. (Courtesy of the Local History Collection, Ellensburg Public Library, Ellensburg, Washington, USA)

George would probably have drunk in Roslyn's famous tavern 'The Brick' (rebuilt in 1898 out of 45,000 bricks), famous for having a running-water spittoon that ran all the way down the length of the main saloon. Miners could enjoy the facilities of a gym, meeting rooms, a bowling alley and a library. Shortly after George arrived in Roslyn in 1909 there was a terrible explosion at Mine No 4 and ten miners died. This may have seemed a small calamity to George after the awful Maypole Pit Disaster that had occurred in Wigan in 1908 – five months before his departure for America – resulting in the loss of seventy-five lives.

Going Native?
But what about the persistent idea that George lived with the Red Indians? An email to the curator of the Roslyn Mining Museum established that the nearest Indian Reservation today is not far away at the Yakama Indian Nation Headquarters at Toppenish, Washington. In Roslyn's early years, the Yakama Indians apparently came through Roslyn regularly on their way to fish for salmon and pick berries in the mountains. Online images of early Roslyn at www.epl.eburg.com/Roslyn/ show Native Americans alongside other cultural groups. My great-grandfather would almost certainly have seen Red Indians, even if the idea that he lived with them – and sold them 'firewater' as family rumour will have it – is perhaps stretching probability a bit far.

There is another possible explanation for the Red Indian legend, as well. I corresponded with the Librarian at Ellensburg Public Library, Ellensburg, Washington, who told me that there was a society known as the 'Red Men Fraternal Organisation' active in Roslyn during the time that George Wilkinson was there. The 'Red Men' (often referred to as 'Red Indians') were a patriotic club of white Americans – one of many fraternities – who, for political purposes, emulated the organisation of the great Iroquois Indian nation. Membership of this society involved playing with the idea of being Indian, taking part in secret ceremonies, donning Indian costumes and adopting coded Indian identities. It's just possible that George's knowledge of Native American culture came from his familiarity with this group.

An Earlier Trip West
Although I now know that George travelled to America as part of a family group, I have been loath to give up the idea of him as a determined

Passenger list showing George Wilkinson's first trip to America in 1893. (www.ancestry.co.uk)

individualist out to seek his fortune in an unknown world. There was one final surprise for me on the 1909 passenger list which has kept the glamour of George still alive. When asked by an official whether or not he had been to America before, my great-grandfather must have replied – to my amazement – in the affirmative. It is recorded on the passenger list that he had made an earlier visit to 'Tex' (Texas) and 'Pa' (Pennsylvania). The date of that earlier trip (or trips) is unclear with the confusing figures '1891/3' being recorded. On the strength of this information, however, I searched the online passenger lists further and found a George Wilkinson of the right age from Hindley making a trip across the Atlantic in 1893. I wonder now whether that was the occasion when he set out West alone and panned for gold. I look forward to finding out!

Carnival Glass

This unusual vase – and its twin sister – are testimony to George's time in America. As a child I used to wonder whether extravagant George (as some of his descendants chose to remember him) had won them at the fair and brought them home in his knapsack as a peace offering for his wife, Mary. The glass has a rainbow sheen – a bit like the way petrol looks on the surface of water. In fact, the internet informed me that the vases are made from a pressed glass that has had an iridised surface treatment. Such glass, initially known as 'Iridill', 'Rubi-glass', or 'dope-glass', was first produced on a large scale by the Fenton Art Glass Company, of Williamstown, West Virginia, but was later made by several other companies across America. 'Carnival' glass, as it later became known, was very popular in America between 1908 and 1918 – exactly the time period when George Wilkinson would have been there. According to the Ellensburg Librarian, general stores in places like Roslyn would have carried glass souvenir items.

'Poor man's Tiffany': one of the vases that George brought home. (Author's collection)

Key Source: Passenger Lists

You need to keep your mind open to various possibilities when researching your emigrant ancestors. There is a common myth that everybody who travelled to America in the last years of the nineteenth century and the first years of the twentieth century arrived in New York and passed through the Ellis Island registration centre. In fact, there were many other ports of entry, including Locust Point in Baltimore Harbour, Angel Island in San Francisco Bay, and Galveston Island at Galveston. Immigrants also arrived in Boston, Philadelphia and New Orleans. Your ancestor might also have departed from a number of different ports in Britain or Ireland (not necessarily the one nearest to his or her home).

How can I find passenger lists relating to trips made by my ancestor?
A number of published volumes may provide you with the details of how to locate your ancestor's shipping record – see 'Resources to Take you Further: Books', below. In addition to these, many passenger lists are now available on line at www.libertyellisfoundation.org, www.ancestry.co.uk and www.findmypast.co.uk.

What can I find out about my ancestor from passenger lists?
This depends very much upon where your ancestor was travelling to and which year he or she was travelling in. The passenger lists for voyages from Liverpool to America made in 1909 (as in this chapter) are particularly rich sources of information including:

- family name
- given [first] name
- age
- sex
- married or single
- calling or occupation
- ability to read or write
- nationality (country of which citizen or subject)
- race or people
- last permanent residence (city or town)
- the name and complete address of nearest relative or friend in country whence alien came
- final destination (state, city or town)
- whether having a ticket to such final destination
- by whom the passage was paid
- whether in possession of $50, and, if less, how much

- whether ever before in the United States and if so, when and where
- whether going to join a relative or friend, and his name and complete address
- whether ever in prison, almshouses or institution for care and treatment of the insane, or supported by charity, if so, which
- whether a polygamist
- whether an anarchist
- whether coming by any offer, solicitation, promise or agreement, express or implied to labour in the United States
- condition of health, mental and physical
- deformed or crippled nature, length of time and cause
- height in feet and inches
- complexion
- colour of hair
- colour of eyes
- marks of identification
- place of birth (country, city or town).

Think laterally

Make sure when looking at passenger lists that you check the names of other people who appear fairly close to your ancestor on the list. You may be surprised to find that rather than travelling alone, as you might romantically have assumed, your ancestor was part of a family group. Check also the home addresses of other non-family members on the list too. Sometimes, whole communities or neighbourhoods from British towns decided to move to America together.

If you want to try to imagine what it was like for your ancestor to travel to America, consider first finding out more about the vessel in which he travelled. The Ellis Island website (www.libertyellisfoundation.org) has pictures of many of the ships that took passengers from Britain to America. To appreciate what a transatlantic journey was really like, consider the length of time your ancestor would have spent aboard ship. In the nineteenth century and up to the First World War, steamships usually took two to three weeks to cross. Sailing ships, on the other hand, took between four to twelve weeks. By the 1920s, steamship times had been reduced to one or two weeks. By the Second World War, journeys took just five days.

Look up the name of your ancestor's destination in an encyclopaedia or in an online encyclopaedia such as www.wikipedia.org. Historical descriptions of cities and towns overseas may contain details which make the reason for your ancestor's journey clear.

Resources to Take You Further
Books
Anuta, Michael J., *Ships of our Ancestors*, Menominee, 1983.

Coleman, Terry, *Passage to America: A History of Emigrants from Great Britain and Ireland to America in the Mid-Nineteenth Century*, Pimlico, 1992.

Colletta, John P., *They Came in Ships: A Guide to Finding Your Immigrant Ancestor's Arrival Record*, Ancestry rpt, 1993.

Filby, William P., *Passenger and Immigration Lists Bibliography 1538-1900: Being a Guide to Published Lists of Arrivals in the United States and Canada*, 2nd edition, Gale Research Co., 1988.

Kershaw, R., *Emigrants and Ex Pats: A Guide to Sources on UK Emigration and Residents Overseas*, PRO, 2000.

Kraut, Alan M., *The Huddled Masses: The Immigrant in American Society, 1880-1921*, Harlan Davidson, 2001.

Novotny, Ann, *Strangers at the Door*, The Chatham Press, 1971.

Shideler, John C., *Coal Towns in the Cascades: A Centennial History of Roslyn and Cle Elum, Washington*, Melior Publications, 1986.

Wittke, Carl F., *We Who Built America: The Saga of the Immigrant*, Western Reserve UP, 1964.

Websites
www.ancestry.co.uk Includes an Immigration and Travel section with millions of passenger records.

www.findmypast.co.uk Includes a Travel and Migration section with millions of passenger records for people leaving the UK.

www.libertyellisfoundation.org Includes a searchable database of more than 51 million records of passengers who entered America through Ellis Island.

www.libertyellisfoundation.org/immigration-museum Ellis Island Immigration Museum.

www.roslynlibrary.org/History.html The history of Roslyn, particularly its coal-mining era.

www.roslynmuseum.com/ Roslyn Historical Museum Society.

www.thecgs.co.uk/ The Carnival Glass Society.

www.understandingyourancestors.com/ia/shipvoyage.aspx Useful detail on how your ancestors might have experienced their journey to America.

www.wigan.gov.uk/Resident/Museums-archives/Wigan-Archives/index.aspx Wigan Archives Service.

www.youtube.com/watch?v=sgFhfmCBIwI Short video of a walking tour around Roslyn, Washington. In the 1990s, the town was the location for the American TV series 'Northern Exposure'.

Addresses
Wigan Archives Service
Leigh Town Hall
Leigh
Wigan
WN7 1DY

Roslyn Mining Museum
203 W. Pennsylvania Avenue
Roslyn
Washington 98941
USA

Local History Collection
Ellensburg Public Library
209, N. Ruby Street
Ellensburg
Washington 98926
USA

CHAPTER 9

'Grandfather Owned a Piece of Gold'

Focus on History: The British Empire and Immigration
Key source: Passports

Many of our recent ancestors came to Britain from overseas. If they came from British colonies or protectorates, their individual stories are probably intimately tied up with the changing fortunes of the British Empire. If you are going to trace your family history from another country, you will ultimately need to understand the way that records were kept in other places. That research is a topic beyond the limits of this book, but one place to start, if you wish to find out more about ancestors from abroad who arrived in Britain at any time since the First World War, may be with the passports they carried. Similarly, if you have ever puzzled about the disappearance of a family member from British records at any time over the past century, it is worth considering that he or she may have been travelling abroad for work or pleasure. Passports may be a rich source of information on many aspects of their lives – particularly where they travelled to and why.

The Story
It's sometimes hard enough to piece together your family tree if your ancestors came from different parts of the British Isles but where on earth do you start, if, as in the case with my husband's family, your ancestors came from other parts of the Empire – in fact from not just one other continent but two? Taibali Essaji Sachak, my husband's grandfather, was a British Protected Person of Tanganyika (now Tanzania) but he was born in India. Amongst his possessions when he died was his last passport (an old, rather weather-beaten document issued in Dar-es-Salaam in 1938) which gives fascinating detail of his extraordinary life lived between three continents: Asia, Africa and Europe.

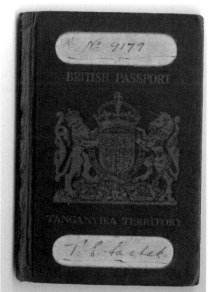

Taibali Essaji Sachak (1891–1944). All later generations of the family have a copy of this photograph of Taibali at work in his office. (Author's collection)

The passport belonging to my husband's grandfather, Taibali Essaji Sachak. (Author's collection)

The few pages of the passport prompted me to quiz my in-laws more closely than I had ever done before in an effort to find out about both my husband's family roots and the history of one of Britain's most vibrant ethnic communities. As well as giving me a lot of information about Taibali's life – the passport also posed a mystery. On an entry visa to Switzerland in December 1939 appear the words: 'Visiter femme et fils' – 'to visit wife and son'. I wondered what this Asian gentleman from Tanganyika had been doing in Switzerland just before the Second World

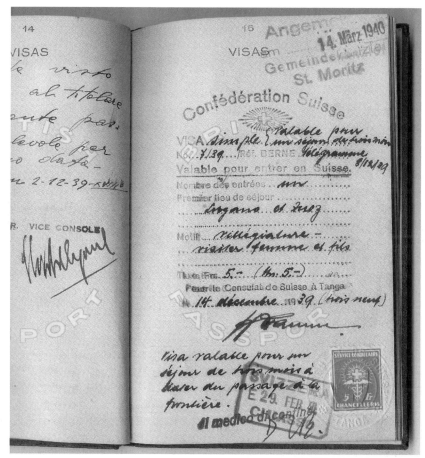

This visa mentions 'a wife and child in Switzerland'. (Author's collection)

War and – more to the point – what was his wife was doing there? As far as I knew, my husband's grandmother, Rukiabai, had never left East Africa.

Your Ancestor's Looks

Perhaps the most exciting thing about passports is that they give you an immediate physical description of your ancestor – details of height and any defining features, for instance. Taibali was 5 foot, 3 inches tall and had 'a mole on his right shoulder'. His signature is assured and artistic, giving the impression of a confident and creative man. Passports (from 1914 onwards) also include photographs. Taibali's shows a serious-looking young man in thick round glasses.

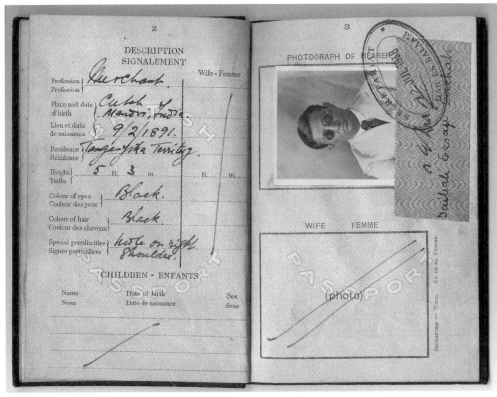

The description page in a passport can yield many different kinds of information, including profession, place of birth, date of birth, details of physical appearance, spouse and children. (Author's collection)

Before I saw the passport, a rather romanticised version of Taibali's life story had been told to me many times over by various family members. Sometimes the tale would be told in Gujarati and interpreted by my husband, but its key features were always the same. A young and poor Taibali had apparently sailed with his uncle from India to Tanganyika in a dhow or 'sewn ship' at some unspecified time in the early years of the twentieth century. On arrival he had started a business selling animal hides in the town of Korogwe. Through hard work and good fortune, he had progressed to owning estates growing something called 'sisal', and by the 1940s, when he died, he was an extremely rich man with a trading empire that stretched as far as Northern Europe.

From Asia to Africa

Indians have always sailed across the Indian Ocean to trade with East Africa. Originally they brought with them such goods as silk, ironware, glass, copperware, pottery, carpets and cloth. From Africa, they brought back copper, gold, ivory, copra (coconut kernels) and coir (coconut fibre) among other things. In the eighteenth and nineteenth centuries, Indians came across the ocean for other reasons too, crossing it first as slaves, then as indentured labourers (at the hands of the colonial governments) and, lastly, after the Indian Emigration Act of 1883, as free workers. In the early years of the twentieth century, young and ambitious Indians like Taibali Sachak were in great demand in the developing colonial economies of East Africa, i.e. Tanganyika Territory (governed, at that point, by the Germans), and Kenya Colony (including parts of modern-day Uganda, governed by the British). Taibali probably sailed from India to Africa between November and March (other evidence suggests this was in 1910) in order to take advantage of the monsoon or 'trade winds'. The journey (of approximately 2,200 miles) would have taken 20–25 sailing days (at other times of year it might have taken months).

Taibali Sachak's passport began to put flesh on the bones of this rags-to-riches saga. Passports tell us not only where their holder resides but also his or her place of birth. Taibali, I discovered, was born on 9 February 1891 in the Indian town of Mandvi in the province of Cutch (sometimes spelt Kutch) in the state of Gujarat on India's Western seaboard. Knowing this fact meant that I could search for some relevant reading material. Lois Lobo's *They Came to Africa: Two Hundred Years of the Asian Presence in Tanzania* (2000), suggested a number of possible reasons for Taibali's migration. These included the massive population explosion in North-West India at the end of the nineteenth century, changing patterns of land tenure under the British Empire (which meant that many Indian families were landless), and extensive joblessness due to the fact that the Gujarat cotton industry had ground to a halt as a result of the importation of cloth from Britain and America. By 1920, about two million Indians had left the land of their birth to seek their fortunes elsewhere. Taibali was evidently among them.

The Merchant Prince

Recently as I was talking to one of my husband's relatives about Taibali, he surprised me by producing a book from his shelves entitled *Asians in East and Central Africa* (1961) by Shanti Pandit. This is no less than a sort of *Who's Who* of Asians in East Africa in the twentieth century. And

— 92 —

He has donated to the Goan Community the Dr. Ribeiro Goan School, Nairobi, and supported many other Goan social institutions.

The Late Mr. T. E. Sachak.
The late Mr. T. E. Sachak who after preliminary education, came in 1910 to Tanga by dhow at the age of 14. After taking a little training in piecegoods trade with his uncle, Mr. Sachak went to Korogwe and started a business of piecegoods, hides and skins in 1910 and throughout the First World War was in business at Korogwe. In 1920 he came to Tanga and started a general business. In 1922 he entered the sisal and kapok industries and very soon began running the following estates :— Ngombezital, Gomba, Ngomeni, & Mombasa Sisal estates. In 1924 he visited Europe in connection with his businesses and opened an office in Germany in 1929 under the name and style of Indian-African Trading Co., MBH, Hamburg. The Founder, Mr. T. E. Sachak. died in 1944 leaving a number of sisal estates and a vast organisation. The business is now run by his sons, Messrs. Shamoonali, Mustafa and Yakubali and they are the present directors.

In Mr. Sachak's loving memory the family have built Taibali Sachak Bohora School, and Rukia Sachak Hostel and donations have been given to various charitable institutions among which are the East African Muslim Welfare Society, The Mombasa Muslim Institute, a Bohora Hostel at Dar-es-Salaam. £5,000 to King Georve VI Memorial in Tanga, and several African Mosques and Schools throughout Tanganyika. In 1952 a building called Sachak House was erected in King Street, Tanga, at a cost of £70,000.

Sachania, Dayaljibhai Pitamber.
Born at Zanzibar in 1913, late Dayaljibhai Sachania became an architect holding the qualification of A.A.S.T.A., (London), after finishing his education in Dhrol and Zanzibar. He first joined the Dhrol State as planning engineer and private secretary to H. H. The Maharaja. While in Dhrol he designed and supervised many state and public buildings including schools, hospitals and markets. Became the District Engineer in Halar Division after the merger of States. Came to Mombasa in 1905 and working with his cousin, Mr M. L. Sachania, went into private practice in Zanzibar. Mr. D. P. Sachania had designed many Government, Public and Private Buildings in Zanzibar. Son of an old pioneer, Dayaljibhai Sachania was very prominent and popular with

Page from a rare book, *Asians in East and Central Africa* by Shanti Pandit (Nairobi, 1961). This includes biographical portraits of key figures in the East African business world, including Taibali Esaaji Sachak. The entry gives Taibali's age on arriving in Tanganiyka as 14. If the passport is to be trusted, he was actually 19. (With thanks to Amir Sachak)

there, on page 92, to my delight was a photograph of Taibali Sachak with a long paragraph of biographical information. There are apparently a number of copies of this book (published in Nairobi in 1961) in the possession of the family but it is otherwise so rare that I have been unable to purchase one over the internet. Within a few sentences, the vagueness that had characterised the oral version of the story was replaced with precise facts. The book gave me, for example, the date of Taibali's arrival in Tanzania (1910), the date of his move from Korogwe to Tanga (1920), and the names of his sisal estates.

What the biographical information didn't tell me was exactly how Taibali had made the transition from seller of hides to man of fortune. The key to finding out more seemed to lie in the word 'sisal' (intoned with reverence by the family). Through internet searches and library books, I learnt that sisal is a stiff fibrous plant which was originally brought to Tanganyika by the German settlers who governed the country from 1891. It was grown and harvested on huge estates by African workers who lived in communities on site.

Taibali's first sisal estate was at Muheza. He gradually added more and more estates to his portfolio: some of these were owned outright and some were managed as 'custodian estates' on behalf of the British. (With thanks to Ruky Sachak)

Workers on one of the sisal estates. (With thanks to Ruky Sachak)

Sisal estates were one of the mainstays of the economy of German East Africa before the First World War. At the end of the war, Tanganyika was mandated by the League of Nations to the British who, uncertain of the future, were not interested in running the estates. Between May 1921 and May 1922, thirty-six sisal estates were put up for auction and bought – at knock-down prices – by Asian merchants. This was exactly the time when – according to the biographical book – Taibali became involved in sisal.

A Cultural Mix

By 1920, the population in Tanganyika was three million Africans, and 24,253 Asians. The ruling Europeans, by contrast, numbered only 9,951. Taibali himself was a Muslim from the Bohra sect. Other Asian settlers were Hindus, Parsis, Jains and Catholics. Arabs had also been settled on the East African seaboard for centuries.

In later life, Taibali told his children that his estates were 'a piece of gold'. He was right: in the middle decades of the twentieth century, sisal was exported to every industrial country for use as ropes, cordage, baling, upholstery, shoes, bags and many other items. Within twenty years, Taibali Sachak had accumulated a vast fortune. Inspired by his success, he branched out into other areas, running, in partnership, a factory that produced soap and edible oil. He later became an agent for the South

British Insurance Company and managed properties. It was at this point that the passport was able to pick up Taibali's story again. The many colourful visas and stamps record a life of international travel and commerce to places as diverse as India, Egypt, Italy and Kenya. Taibali was also a frequent visitor to Britain (he had an agent in London) and Germany (he had an office in Hamburg) in the years immediately preceding the Second World War.

And So to Europe
But what of the passport's mention of Taibali's 'wife and son' in Switzerland? I knew that he had married Rukiabai (Mulla Adamjee) in 1917 and that they had had six children. From everything I had heard about her, I knew that Rukiabai was no international traveller. Further discussions with the family enlightened me. By the end of the 1930s, Taibali's frequent business trips to Europe meant that he was away for nearly half of each year. He needed companionship and this had resulted in his taking – with the blessing of his family back in Tanganyika – a second wife (something that was not inconsistent with his Muslim faith). Emily (a German woman) converted to Islam and was renamed Amina. With the outbreak of the Second World War, Taibali and Amina moved to Switzerland to be out of the reach of the Nazis. The 'son' mentioned in the visa was not a child of Amina's, but was in fact Taibali and Rukiabai's eldest son, Shamun, who, in 1939, was being educated in Switzerland.

The passport yielded one important final piece of information: a stamp, obtained in November 1941 for a trip to India, and a second stamp, issued in April 1942 for a return journey to Tanganyika. This was a long sojourn away from Taibali's business interests. I wondered why. Again, the family's memories were prompted. Taibali was suffering from tuberculosis at this time and was advised to seek treatment in Bombay. The Indian doctor later returned with him to Tanga but, despite his best efforts, Taibali died two years later. He was just 53.

In 1961 Tanganyika gained independent status within the British Commonwealth and, uniting with the island of Zanzibar, the country took a new name 'Tanzania'. Under President Nyerere, the African majority came to power and the sisal estates were nationalised in 1967. Like many other Asian families, in the early 1970s, the Sachaks found their position in a socialist country untenable. Eventually, they took advantage of their grandfather's old links with Europe and migrated again. Some went to

Typical pages in the passport. (Author's collection)

Switzerland to be educated while others – including my husband, his parents and his brothers – came to Britain.

Taibali's tale is one of extraordinary personal endeavour and talent. It is also a telling example of a family's history in which huge changes in personal fortune occurred as a direct result of the rise and fall of the British Empire.

Key Source: Passports

A passport is a document that identifies the individual holding it and allows this individual entry to another geographical area as well as permitting return to the point of origin. Passports, letters of transit and similar documents were used for centuries to allow individuals to travel safely in foreign lands, but the adoption of the passport by all nations is a development of the eighteenth and nineteenth centuries. The story of the modern passport really began at the end of the First World War (in 1914) when most European states and their colonial outposts tightened or reinforced passport requirements. The British Nationality and Status Aliens Act came into force in 1915. As a result, the modern mandatory passport was born. This was a one-page printed document with a cardboard cover and a photograph. It was valid for two years and could be renewed for two further two-year periods.

In 1920, The League of Nations International Conference on Passports, Customs Formalities and Through Tickets, and later the United Nations and International Civil Aviation Organisation, issued standard guidelines on the layout and features of passports. These guidelines have largely shaped the modern passport. At this time, a 32-page book format for passports was introduced. This became known as the 'Old Blue'.

Where can I get hold of details of passports issued to citizens of British colonies?
If you do not have your ancestor's actual passport, you may be able to find records (containing basic information about your ancestor at the time it was issued) in archives held in the country where it was issued. For records of passports issued to citizens of British colonies, you should contact the British High Commission in those places. The supporting information to individual passport applications is usually destroyed after twelve years, but basic information about the application may remain.

The British High Commission in Tanzania (see address below in 'Resources to Take You Further: Addresses') holds basic records of passports issued to British Protected Persons in the 1950s and 1960s.

Passports issued in the UK
In the UK, passport records are held centrally within the Identity and Passport Service at Peterborough and in regional passport locations. If you wish to find out about a passport issued since 1898, you should send a certified copy of your ancestor's death certificate, some identification of your own (either your own current passport or a utility bill) together with details of the information you are looking for to:

Disclosure of Information
Her Majesty's Passport Office
Aragon Court
Northminster Road
Peterborough
PE1 1QG

The Peterborough office houses the records of all the regional passport offices plus records of British passports issued abroad. Old passports themselves have not been retained and supporting documentation will have been destroyed after twelve years. What have been kept, however, are index cards (now in microfiche format) of the details of passports issued. The information held on these cards is as follows: names; the place and date of birth of the passport holder (and any persons included in that passport); the passport number; place and date of issue; and (after 1963), details of nationality status. Unfortunately, no photographs have been retained, and there are, of course, no records of where your ancestor actually travelled.

The National Archives at Kew also holds some (incomplete) information about passports issued in Britain. See www.national archives.gov.uk/help-with-your-research/research-guides/passports for more detail. This gives detail of an online register of Passport Applications from 1851 to 1903 (which has some gaps); and of indexes, registers and case papers relating to passports which, between them, cover the longer period 1795 to 1983 and which can be viewed at the Archives.

What can a passport tell me about my ancestor?
The forms that allow you to obtain a passport were filled out by the applicant, signed by him or her, and witnessed. The information within them, therefore, is likely to be more accurate than that in census records, birth, marriage and death certificates and obituaries. An 'Old Blue Passport' will give you:

• family name
• given name
• place of birth
• date of birth
• occupation
• country of residence
• national status
• spouse
• children (until 1998 included in the passport of one or other of their parents)
• height
• distinguishing features. On early twentieth-century passports, this is a
   written description. The shape of the face might be described as 'round'

144

or 'oval', the complexion as 'fair' or 'dark', and some features might also be described (for example, forehead: broad or medium; nose: large, straight; eyes: small, mouth: medium. Passports may also comment on the presence of a beard or moustache, the shape of the chin (round), and the colour of the hair ('dark', 'black' or 'fair'). It can be delightful to find comments written in the 'special peculiarities' section of your ancestor's passport e.g. 'spectacles worn' or 'mole on the right shoulder.

• signature
• photographs (from 1914 onwards). These tend to be clearer than family snaps since the applicant had to sit squarely facing the camera. They also have to be validated as a *true likeness* of the applicant by someone of professional standing.
• signature of a witness
• names and addresses of two relatives or friends who can be contacted in case of an emergency
• records of the exchange of foreign currency on the holder's return to Britain.

Think laterally

Passports will record an ancestor's travels with colourful visas and stamps. A visa is a document issued by a country giving a certain individual permission to formally request entrance to the country during a given period of time and for certain purposes. Visas can tell you where a member of your family travelled and give you some idea of how long they were away from home. But, be careful here – the length of period for which the visa is valid is not necessarily the period for which your ancestor was away. The dates on a visa can, however, give you some useful parameters of time between which he or she might have been out of the country. A visa will usually be accompanied by a stamp; this may give you the exact date of an ancestor's arrival in another country.

Look out for other bits and pieces of information collected between the pages of passports. One belonging to one of my ancestors, for example, contained several vaccination certificates and stamps detailing inoculations against cholera, yellow fever, typhoid and smallpox. You may also find copies of documents that would originally have accompanied a passport application, for example, supporting letters and affidavits from friends or relatives concerning the applicant's citizenship status, residence, and character.

Resources to Take You Further

Books

Ghai, Dharam P., *Portrait of a Minority: Asians in East Africa*, Oxford U.P., 1965.

Hollingsworth, Lawrence William, *The Asians of East Africa*, Macmillan, 1960.

Kershaw, R. and Pearsall, M., *Immigrants and Aliens: A Guide to Sources on UK Immigration and Citizenship*, PRO, 2000.

Lloyd, Martin, *The Passport: The History of Man's Most Travelled Document*, Sutton Publishing, 2003.

Lobo, Lois, *They Came to Africa: Two Hundred Years of the Asian Presence in Tanzania*, Sustainable Village, 2000.

Mangat, J. S., *A History of Asians in East Africa c 1886-1945*, Clarendon, 1969.

Mbogani, Lawrence E. Y., *Aspects of Colonial Tanzania History*, Mkuki Na Nyota Publishers, 2013.

Pandit, Shanti, *Asians in East and Central Africa*, Nairobi, 1961.

Seidenberg, Dana April, *Mercantile Adventurers: The World Of East African Asians, 1750-1985*, New Age International Publishers, 1986.

Torpey, John, *The Invention of the Passport: Surveillance, Citizenship and the State*, Cambridge University Press, 2000.

Visram, Rosina, *Asians in Britain: 400 Years of History*, Pluto Press, 2002.

Websites

www.bbc.co.uk/asiannetwork/africaweek/memoriesofafrica.shtml Oral testimonials of Asians from East Africa on the BBC Asian network.

www.bbc.co.uk/news/world-africa-14095868 A chronology of Tanzania's history.

www.channel4.com/programmes/empires-children Site including the stories of British celebrities whose lives were affected by the dismantling of the British Empire.

www.gov.uk/browse/abroad/passports Information about British passports.

www.nationalarchives.gov.uk/catalogue/RdLeaflet.asp?sLeafletID=109 &j=1 Information on passports and passport information held in the National Archives.

www.nationalarchives.gov.uk/records/looking-for-person/passport.htm Information from the National Archives about how to search for an ancestor's passport.

www.ntz.info/ A forum for people who live or have lived in Northern Tanzania.

www.scan.org.uk/familyhistory/myancestor/passport.htm On obtaining the passport of an ancestor from Scotland.

www.untoldlondon.org.uk/ The history of London's diverse communities.

www.webarchive.nationalarchives.gov.uk/+/http:/www.movinghere.org.uk/ The Moving Here website collected testimony of 200 years of the history of migration to the UK. This site is no longer receiving material. It has now been archived by the National Archives, but can still be searched online.

Addresses
British High Commission
Umoja House
Hamburg Avenue
P.O. Box 9200
Dar-es-Salaam

National Archives of Tanzania
POB 2006
Vijibweni Street
Dar-es-Salaam
Tanzania

Tanzanian Embassy
Consulate Section
3, Stratford Place
London
W1C 1AS

CHAPTER 10

'She Supported the Family'

Focus on History: Domestic Service
Key Source: Oral History

It is often the case that you will find out more about the lives of the fathers, sons, brothers, and uncles in your family than the women. This is only to be expected: the males in families more often worked in the public sphere, took positions of prominence in local communities and churches, committed crimes and acted as the signatories of documents – all of which make them more visible than women in written records. To piece together the lives of your grandmothers, great-grandmothers and their sisters, you will need to think laterally and use other kinds of sources including oral history. Women were traditionally the singers and tellers of tales in families. Consider whether any songs or ditties been passed down through the generations and whether they can tell you anything about your

My grandfather didn't want to associate his beautiful mother with the menial task of washing. (Author's collection)

origins. And when you speak to any member of the older generation, listen carefully to the way they speak – traces of accents, odd words and phrases, rhymes and riddles may all betray their past.

The Story

> Ee, I'd love give thee a cup of tay [tea]
> If tha'd only come on th'reet [right] day
> But tha' maughn't [mustn't] come on a Monday,
> Monday's washin' day,

I'll be washin' an' washin'
All't clothes away.

Ee I'd love give thee a cup o 'tay
If tha'd only come on th'reet day
But tha maughn't come on a Tuesday,
Tuesday's ironin' day,
I'll be ironin' an' ironin'
All't clothes away.
. . . etc

'Monday is washing day'. Washday, Wigan, 1891. (With thanks to Ron Hunt)

'When you're married and in the tub'. Wigan, 1890s. (With thanks to Ron Hunt)

I remember singing this old Lancashire song as a child. My grandmother taught it to me and she had learned it from her mother-in-law, my great-grandmother, Mary Wilkinson (née Knowles). It tells the tale of a woman who would love to share a cup of tea with her friend, but just can't find the time. On Mondays and Tuesdays she spends the whole day washing and ironing and, judging by the woefulness of her complaint, the laundering is a substantial load – not just her own but probably, that of others too. Also, when my grandmother signed my childhood autograph book, she included another washing song that had been passed down through the family from her mother-in-law.

When you're married and in the tub
Think o' me between every rub
Be the soapsuds ever so hot
Lather away and forget me not.

Two songs about washing? Was this just a co-incidence or were there clues here to the life of my great-grandmother? It was only after singing these two songs for many years, that I put them together with another fragment of evidence. I remembered that my grandfather, Mary's son, once told me, rather embarrassedly, that his mother used to 'take in washing'. He could remember vividly the smell of carbolic soap and lime dominating their terraced home in Wigan, Lancashire. I suddenly realised that Mary Wilkinson had been a washerwoman who was paid for her efforts, and not just a housewife who had plenty of washing to do. These must have been the songs with which she used to while away the hours of bleaching and washing, wringing and drying.

The Work of Women

I went to have a look at the 1901 census online to see if I could find any evidence of Mary's working life, but I was disappointed. At 34 years old and married with three children, my great-grandmother is recorded with no occupation, and it looks as though her family were entirely reliant for their income on the wages of her husband, George, a coal hewer at one of the collieries in Wigan. Somehow, it seemed quite unjust that Mary's washing business was not recorded. It had, after all, supported an entire family at times.

Mary Wilkinson in her washing clothes, early 1930s. The strap on her arm indicates that she may have injured it from the repeated mangling and wringing-out of clothes. (Author's collection)

Mary Wilkinson on the 1901 census where she is recorded as having no occupation. (www.ancestry.co.uk)

> **Men's and Women's Employment on the Census**
> It is usually quite easy to find out what the men in a family did in the past. Paid, full-time employment outside the home, such as coalmining, labouring or blacksmithing, is recorded quite clearly on the census. But researching the working life of a married woman is quite a different matter. Faced with a blank space in the 'occupations' box, you can easily assume, quite wrongly, that your female ancestor didn't work at all. This is particularly true if your grandmother or great-grandmother did piecemeal, non-unionised, quasi-domestic work – such as laundering, charring or laying out the dead. One of the reasons for this is that working-class men were often reluctant to admit to the census enumerators that their womenfolk needed to work.

I wondered if I could find out more about Mary's working life by looking back into her past, to the time before she was married. Her birth certificate told me that she was the daughter of a small-time farmer, Richard Knowles, in Westhoughton near Bolton. As farm jobs for girls were growing scarcer and scarcer in the late nineteenth century, Mary started out in the world of work not on her father's four acres, but as a 'knotter in a cotton factory'. Since this job was outside the home, it was accorded the dignity of an entry on the 1881 census when Mary was just fourteen. Ten years later, by the time of the 1891 census, Mary was – somewhat surprisingly – no longer living at her father's address. I did a search on the census online for her maiden name (Mary Knowles) and age (24), and was delighted to find her living at the rather grandly-named 'Laburnum Villa', Pilkington Street, Hindley, Wigan – a far more elegant address than I had expected. It appeared that my great-grandmother's career had changed: she was now working as a 'general servant' and living in the home of a family named Lowe – (Thomas (63), his wife Ellen (63), and their two grandchildren Ellen (13) and John (11)).

I wondered whether my great-grandmother had found cotton knotting repetitive, or if she had simply preferred to work in the familiar surroundings of a family home rather than a public building. Whatever the case, at some point in the 1880s, she left the mill for a residential position in the Lowe's family home. A couple of library books (including

Mary Knowles is described as a 'General Servant' on the 1891 census. (www.ancestry.co.uk)

Pamela Horn's *On the Rise and Fall of the Domestic Servant* (Sutton 1986) on the history of domestic service helped me to fill in a little background at this point. From these, I learned that Mary's move from factory work into domestic service was actually somewhat unusual. Factory pay was reasonably good by the end of the nineteenth century and legislation had reduced working hours to a reasonable level. Because of this, there were far fewer servants in northern textile towns like Wigan than there were in older towns and cities.

Domestic Servants

By the 1880s, around a third of all young women between the ages of 15 and 21 were likely to be in service and this corresponded with a sharp rise in the numbers of families able to afford resident domestic staff. A majority of three-fifths of all servants were employed, like Mary Knowles, not as part of large retinues in big stately homes, but as 'maids-of-all work' in the homes of small tradesmen such as drapers, plumbers and coal merchants. Mr Lowe of Laburnum Villa was a retired grocer and having Mary working for him would have been an important sign of social respectability. To be able to employ Mary, he probably had an annual income of something between £150 and £300. Had he been a professional man, earning up to £1,000 a year, he would have had at least three servants, each with specialist tasks. As it was, Mary probably worked very hard, taking on the duties of housemaid, parlourmaid, nursemaid, kitchenmaid, cook and laundrymaid as the need arose.

Mary's employer, grocer's wife Ellen Lowe, like thousands of other middle-class women in the late nineteenth century, would have spent her time supervising and managing her household rather than doing the practical tasks of housework herself. Mary would have had many duties and, in order to find out more about what these might have been, I looked at an old manual of household work and management from roughly the period in question Annie Butterworth, *Manual of Household Work and Management* (Longman's Green and Co., 1913, pp. 27–33). Such advice books can often be found in second-hand bookshops and they are a fund of fascinating information. In addition to the constant round of daily obligations, Mary would have emptied the slops, blackleaded the grates, cleaned the utensils, and done some of the household mending for the Lowes.

General Servant Duties: House of Seven Rooms

6 a.m. – Rise, light kitchen fire, fill kettle, clean boots, sweep hall, clean steps and brasses, light breakfast- or dining-room fire, sweep and dust the room.

8 a.m. – Prepare and lay cloth for breakfast, have kitchen breakfast while dining room breakfast is going on, open bedroom windows, strip beds, and attend to washstands.

9 a.m. – Remove and wash breakfast-things.

9.20 a.m. – Help mistress to make beds, dust rooms and stairs, receive orders for the day.

10 to 12 a.m. – Special allotted work. The mistress during these hours is probably doing the cooking.

12 to 1 p.m. – Help mistress in the kitchen, lay table for dinner.

1 p.m. – Dining-room and kitchen dinner.

1.30 p.m. – Remove and wash dinner things, knives and saucepans, make up sitting-room fire, tidy kitchen.

2.30 p.m. – Dress, and do some light work, such as cleaning silver; being in readiness to answer the front-door bell.

4.30 p.m. – Prepare tea for [sitting] room and kitchen.

5.15 p.m. – Remove and wash tea things.

5.45 p.m. – Turn down beds, draw bedroom blinds, light gas.

8 p.m. – Prepare supper.

9 p.m. – Remove and wash supper things.

9.45 p.m. – Take hot water to rooms, and go to bed.

From Annie Butterworth, *Manual of Household Work and Management*, Longmans, Green, and Co., 1913, pp. 27–30.

Mary most probably learnt her washerwoman skills in the home of the Lowes. My manual of household management described laundry work as a serious business occupying at least a couple of days a week, and one for which 'early rising [was] essential'. Servants would often be asked to start by entering the clothes they had been given into a 'washing book' in case they later went missing. Then came the job of sorting: table linen, body and bed linen, handkerchiefs, bedroom and bath towels, toilet covers, linen aprons, muslins, kitchen and pantry towels, dusters, prints and flannels, required a variety of different treatments. There followed a complicated process of steeping, washing, boiling, rinsing, blueing, starching and wringing, not to mention drying, damping, ironing, airing and folding!

Work after marriage

I have not been able to find out how long Mary lived with the Lowes. For many women, domestic service was seen as a stage in life – between

155

A new-fangled idea: the Paragon Washer, Wringer and Mangler was made locally. This advert dates from 1881. (With thanks to Ron Hunt)

school and marriage – rather than a full-time career prospect and, at 24, Mary would probably have been considered to be quite old to be still a residential servant in her employer's home. Many servants aspired to marry above their status and Mary may have hoped that, having learnt the middle-class family's so-called 'standards of propriety, cleanliness and order', she would meet a tradesman, shopkeeper or skilled craftsman and go up in the world. As it was, she ended up marrying George Wilkinson – a coalminer – in August 1891.

As was the custom, Mary would probably have left her employment with the Lowes on her marriage. Soon afterwards, she and George started a family. Unfortunately, in 1893, their eldest child, Janette, died at the age of just two from meningitis. Four more children, Wilfred (b. 1896), Elsie (b. 1897), Alf (b. 1899) and George (b. 1904) followed. But despite his growing brood, George was impatient for adventure and left Wigan to work in America as a miner in 1909 (see Chapter 8).

Back in Wigan, however, and without an income of any kind, Mary was forced to resurrect the laundering skills that she had learnt during her time as a general servant. Her home would have smelt not just of carbolic but of starch, turpentine and ammonia as she worked her way through the washing of clients such as her former employers, the Lowes. It is impossible to say how much Mary would have earned from this part-time work, but my library books suggest that, at the end of the nineteenth century, a likely fee for a washerwomen was 'two shillings a day and a meal of bread and cheese'.

When her husband George came back from America, Mary welcomed him with open arms. She continued to 'take in washing' through all the vicissitudes of her husband's working life and through other losses including the death of Wilfred, her eldest son, who was killed during the First World War in Northern France just after his 21st birthday. She never

Two ornaments like this belonged to my great-grandmother. The Bisque pottery seems somewhat too delicate and expensive for the home of a mining family. My mother remembered that these were given to Mary whilst she was working as a residential domestic servant at Laburnum Villa, Wigan. Perhaps she once dusted them on her employers' mantelpiece. (Author's collection)

got over that. I now realise that a census entry could never have captured the arduousness and pathos of Mary's situation. The ditties, passed down through the female generations of the family, on the other hand, have ensured that she and her toil will always be remembered.

Key Source: Oral History
Clues to your family history may be present in all kinds of oral evidence from songs, and rhymes to proverbs, sayings or even mere isolated phrases and words. Any aspect of language that strikes you as odd or unusual is worth scrutinising more carefully. Language is at is most interesting (and may reveal most about family history) where it is metaphorical – that is, where a picture is painted in words. Many proverbs and euphemisms are known by just about everybody in Britain, but there may be some that you have only heard within your own family. If these sayings are not common in the local area, you should consider them as all the more interesting.

What should I look for in particular?
There are certain language topics that are particularly revealing of regional origins. One of these is the weather. When it looks as though it's going to rain hard, do your family say, 'It's syling down' (a Yorkshire expression); 'It's a bit black over Bill's mother's' (a Black Country expression); or that it will 'stoat [i.e. bounce] off the ground' (a Scots expression)?

Some of the other topics which have historically been expressed very differently in the various parts of Britain are:

• eating
• getting drunk
• going to the toilet
• having sex
• the devil
• swearing
• the police

What can I learn about my ancestors from oral history?
The way people speak, or spoke, including their accent, their pronunciation and their choice of words can give away a great deal including:

- which country they came from. Irish immigrants to England brought with them such colourful phrases as 'don't give cherries to pigs or advice to fools', and 'a dimple in the chin; a devil within'. Your family proverbs may have been translated from other languages and may hence sound a little clumsy in English. Italian ancestors, for example, might have used the phrase, 'When the wine is in, the wit is out' and people of Czech origin might have remarked that, 'he who cannot cut the bread evenly cannot get on with people'.
- which region of Britain they came from. 'Rags to riches to rags' is a Lancashire phrase warning that upward social mobility won't last. Yorkshire determination reveals itself in the proverb: 'A pair of spurs to a borrowed horse is better than a peck of oats'. And neighbourly prejudice is betrayed in the Manx remark: 'An eel by his tale, an Irishman at his word.'
- their religious and cultural beliefs. 'The bell, book and candle', are commonly referred to by those of Catholic heritage even if they are no longer devout. Your Jewish ancestry may reveal itself in odd words such as 'chutzpah' (meaning 'cheek') or 'schlep' (meaning 'drag') or in proverbs such as 'worries go down better with soup than without', or you shouldn't 'pick up a wasp out of a jug of cream'. Hindu ancestors may have passed down the advice, 'Dig your well before you are thirsty'. Look out for omissions too: in a Jewish household the word 'God' will not be uttered.
- their occupations (for example, maritime or the military). If your family describe people as 'sulky as bulls', or 'ugly enough to wean a foal', it's possible that they descend from a farming background!
- their level of education and class background (conversation that is unwittingly peppered with references to Shakespeare or nineteenth-century poets may, for instance, suggest ancestors who had a good education).

Think laterally
As well as proverbs, think about euphemisms (ways of expressing something unpalatable or embarrassing). For instance, what phrases do people in your family use to express the fact that someone has died? My Lancashire grandfather used to say, 'He's cocked his toes up'. Catholic ancestors may have used the phrase 'He's kneeling at the big gates'. If

your ancestors used the phrase 'crossing the bar', it may indicate that they were educated types since this is a quotation from the Victorian poet Alfred Lord Tennyson.

As well as listening carefully to the way members of the older generation speak, think about the other ways in which oral culture may have been passed down. Many ditties, for example, appear in written form in guest books and autograph books.

There is a limit to what you can learn from odd phrases and sayings. Many phrases that were once regional or perhaps appropriate to just one profession are now used by everyone. Nevertheless, just thinking about the way your family speak or spoke can suggest all sorts of ideas about their background.

Resources to Take You Further

Books

Butterworth, Annie, *Manual of Household Work and Management*, Longmans, Green, and Co., 1913.

Cullwick, Hannah, *The Diaries of Hannah Cullwick: Victorian Maidservant*, Rutgers UP, 1984.

Higgs, Michelle, *Tracing Your Servant Ancestors*, Pen and Sword, 2012.

Horn, Pamela, *The Rise and Fall of the Domestic Servant*, Alan Sutton, 1986.

Lethbridge, Lucy, *Servants: A Downstairs View of Twentieth-Century Britain*, Bloomsbury, 2013.

May, Trevor, *The Victorian Domestic Servant*, Shire, 1999.

Maloney, Alison, *Life Below Stairs: True Lives of Edwardian Servants*, Michael O'Mara, 2011.

Roberts, Elizabeth, *A Woman's Place: An Oral History of Working-Class Women, 1890-1940*, Blackwell, 1986.

Ward, Margaret, *The Female Line: Researching Your Female Ancestors*, Countryside Books, 2003.

Websites

www.bbc.co.uk/history/british/victorians/womens_work_01.shtml BBC history site on women's work in the nineteenth century.

www.history.ac.uk/makinghistory/resources/articles/oral_history.html How oral history has been used to write history.

www.le.ac.uk/emoha/emoha/arounduk.html List of useful organisations and projects concerned with oral history around the UK.

www.lse.ac.uk/library/collections/featuredCollections/womensLibraryL
SE.aspx The Women's Library at the LSE, documenting women's
lives (particularly in the UK) and the great political, economic and
social changes of the last 150 years.
www.ohs.org.uk The Oral History Society.
www.quotationspage.com Usefully lists quotations by topic giving
some idea of their origins.
www.sounds.bl.uk/accents-and-dialects Accents and sounds in the
British Library Sounds Archive.
www.wcml.org.uk The Working Class Movement Library.

Addresses
The Working Class Movement Library
51, The Crescent
Salford
Manchester
M5 4WX

The Women's Library
4th Floor, Lionel Robbins Building
London School of Economics
Houghton Street
London
WC2A 2AE

CHAPTER 11

'He Always Had His Nose in a Book'

Focus on History: Cultural Tastes and Family Relationships
Key Source: Books and the Family Bible

If ever you come to inherit a hoard of family books, think twice before you donate them to the local charity shop – they may contain clues of many kinds about your ancestors. Ask yourself first what kind of books they are: novels or practical manuals? Boys' stories or early feminist manifestos? Methodist hymnbooks or collections of satirical cartoons? Just by casting your eye along a row of book spines, you can get a vivid impression of an ancestor's interests and preoccupations. A collection of books – their variety and even the quality of their bindings – can also give you other ideas about a relative: his wealth and status, for example, as well indeed, as his level of education. And once you dip inside these precious tomes, you may find much more to interest you.

My father, William Symes (1928–2000). (Author's collection)

'Give me a bookcase and I'll show you the man': collections of books can give away a lot of secrets. (Author's collection)

The Story

My mother would remark with pride, my grandfather with disdain, that my father 'always had his nose in a book'. After he died in 2000, I inherited all those old books. For a long time, I couldn't bear to move them from the shelves on which my father had arranged them. Each had their place, and even their position on the shelves told me something about when he had last read them, and how much he valued them. When I first acquired the books, my father's personality, unassuming but well-informed, seemed to emanate from every title and I hesitated about consigning them to Oxfam. As it happened, it was a good thing I did pause, because on opening them, I was amazed to find that they were full of other sorts of clues about my father's life, and about the lives of other branches and generations of the family.

The volumes are a motley bunch: blue- and orange-spined Penguins, the complete works of Proust and Dickens and a miscellany of coffee-table heritage books. Each decade of my father's life is represented, with a burgeoning of volumes from his university days and from the period after he retired. In a strange way, these books have provided me with a history of my father's life – almost from beginning to end.

The make-up of the collection, for instance, records special moments in my father's life. I found volumes that he must have bought whilst away from home on occasion – a copy of *Oliver Twist*, for example, purchased – it said on the flyleaf – when he visited York in 1942, and a legal textbook from a trip to London made in 1955. There were, as well, books that he had acquired to mark important events. Laurie Lee's *The Firstborn* – which is a short description of Lee's feelings on the birth of his daughter – was bought on my birth in 1966. *A Grief Observed* (a book on bereavement) by C. S. Lewis was purchased at the time that my grandfather died in 1968. I was fascinated by the way in which the books seemed to act as a barometer of events in the family and to confirm – and in some cases supplement – details that I already knew from other documents.

Bookplates and enclosures

But once I opened the books, there was much more to enjoy. Some of them had originally been the school prizes of my father's parents, aunts and uncles in the late nineteenth and early twentieth centuries and included bookplates from schools and Sunday schools in Manchester and York where these relatives had been educated. From a clue on a bookplate in one of my father's books, I was able to locate a churchyard in Heworth, York, in which many family members were buried. As well as alerting you to the fact that your ancestor was good at a particular subject such as geography or maths, bookplates can tell you more about where he or she lived, what religious denomination he or she belonged to, and at which church he or she might have attended services. Other plates in books may indicate your ancestor's membership of numerous different kinds of organisation from temperance societies to trade unions – all of which may have their own searchable records.

My father's collection of books revealed one or two tangible family history clues as well. Between the pages of a much loved book of poetry was his certificate of baptism (at Liverpool Undenominational Church on 16 May 1928). This was a piece of information about him that I had been unable to find among other family papers. As anyone who frequents second-hand bookshops will know, in the past, the insides of books were one of the few places in the house where documents such as birth, marriage and death certificates, letters and wills could be kept flat and dry. Look out for non-documentary enclosures in books as well: flowers picked and pressed on holidays, locks of hair and even pieces of material kept after the making of an important garment can all add detail to the story of how a life was lived.

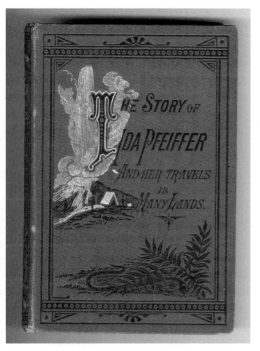
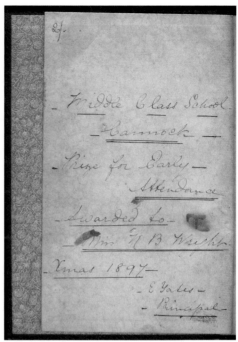

Ida Pfeiffer, *The Story of Ida Pfeiffer and her Travels in Many Lands*, T. Nelson and Sons, 1884. The inscription reads: Middle Class School, Cannock, Prize for Early Attendance. Awarded to Miss N. B. Wright. Xmas 1897, E. Yates, Principal.

Marginalia and inscriptions

And then, of course, there were the doodles, the scribbles, the jottings in the margins – so annoying if you are trying to resell a book, but sometimes so revealing of the people who once owned the volume. On the blank pages behind the pictures in an old nineteenth-century annual, *The Family Friend*, in my father's collection, I found numerous attempts to write names and addresses made by several children in my family probably in the 1880s. It's worth remembering that books may have provided the only bits of spare paper in the home of your ancestor and that children, in particular, must, therefore, sometimes have been tempted to write in them. Most usually, idle doodling involves recording information that can be vitally important to family historians (i.e. signatures, ages, addresses and dates of birth). If you are trying to put a date to scribbles, consider carefully the writing implements that have been used. Bear in mind that ballpoint pens were not in common use until the Second World War.

Handwriting and history

Take a good look at the handwriting of your forebears to see if you can work out clues to their personality. Graphology, is of course, a pseudo-science, but as a quick guide on how to analyse writing, you should try to describe to yourself how it looks. Is it, for example, artistic and daring, or small and careful? Turn the page upside down and describe the writing again. Handwriting is believed by some to mirror the characteristics of personality, so you may come to understand more about the kind of person your ancestor was by this method.

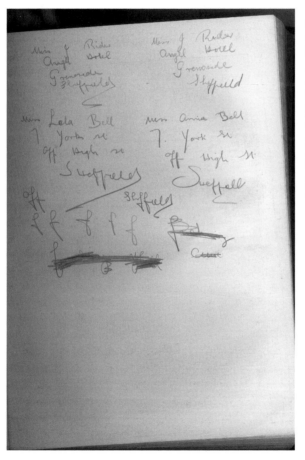

Children's scribblings on a blank page behind a picture in *The Girl's Own Annual, 1886.* The names and addresses of Miss J. Ryder, Miss Lola Bell and Miss Annie Bell – all of Sheffield – can clearly be seen. (*The Girl's Own Annual,* The Leisure Hour Office, 1886)

I looked carefully through each and every one of my father's books for his handwritten notes, arrows and underlinings. Different sorts of books had inspired different sorts of annotation. In the few travel books, he had added his own comments on places visited and dates upon which journeys were made. In political biographies, I found an occasional scrawled remark of disagreement or approval. 'Feminist nonsense' was one comment I discovered beside a passage about women's role in the economy (though I'm hoping that it wasn't penned by my father!). Local history books were particularly interesting since the annotations in these pointed to specific geographical features of my father's life. In one book on the history of Liverpool, for instance, he had drawn a large cross on an aerial photograph to mark the street where he lived. On one or two occasions, my father had gone so far as to evaluate books in their entirety inside the front cover. Comments such as 'Poorly written', or 'Not as good as his last' gave me an insight into how his values, tastes and opinions had developed over the years.

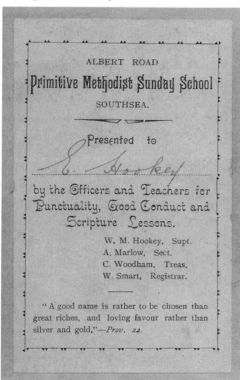

Bookplate indicating that the owner attended the Primitive Methodist Church, Southsea. (Maria Edgeworth, *Popular Tales*, George Routledge, nineteenth century but undated)

So much for what my inherited pile of books could tell me about one individual – my father – but, as books were often given as presents from one family member to another, they were also able to tell me something about the relationships between my ancestors. A handwritten inscription to my father from 'Aunty Annie in Scarborough, 1954', for instance, was enough to enable me to fill in the missing name on a branch of my family tree. And another, fuller, inscription to my grandmother Alice Symes (née Gillings) was even more useful in helping me to name and date her two brothers, my great-uncles.

To our dear little sister, Alice.
Lots of love on your tenth birthday,
from your brothers Walter and Harry,
November 2nd 1904.

A Tale in an Inscription

Some inscriptions are so intricately and affectionately written that they tell a story in themselves. A book held by the National Library of Scotland has the following inscription on its flyleaf.

Lieut. Geo. McDonell of the Invernessshire Militia to Miss Mary McAskill in token of his great regard for that young lady which for a long time could not be made public. Remain my lovely girl. Your new admirer and well-wisher unto death. Geo. McDonell, Lieut. Inverness Militia
(http://www.nls.uk/privatelivesofbooks/inscriptions2.html)

Such a detailed inscription would provide a family historian with a clear insight into the story behind an important family courtship. It might also provide a lead to searchable military records.

Finally, my father's books solved a mystery about his life that I had long puzzled over. Like many mid twentieth-century readers proud to own their own books rather than borrow them from the library, he actually wrote his name and where he was living at the time he was reading each one inside the cover of each volume. I was gratified to find that the collection took me through all his addresses from his being a boy in Liverpool in the 1930s right through evacuation to Bangor, North Wales

(1939–40), and National Service in Germany (1952–4), until he moved to Warrington as a young solicitor in the late 1950s. Here, in a sense, was his whole biography laid out chronologically before me without me having to do anything but put the books in order.

I knew some of my father's addresses already but there had been gaps in my knowledge, particularly of a period of about two years between 1956 and 1958 when his family moved from their home above a shoe shop in the district of Walton, Liverpool, to some unspecified address. Later, they moved back to Walton. I remember my father talking about this period, but I had no details about where he lived during the missing years. Among the pile of books I inherited was a novel that my father had bought and read in 1957 and, to my delight, there on the inside cover was the elusive address – a suburban house in Netherton, Liverpool.

Library Books

Stamps and stickers in books that originated from a library may give you some indication of the towns and districts where your ancestors lived.

It is important to remember that whilst others may enjoy reading your inherited collection of books, the family history information inside them will only ever be of real interest to your family. So, before you cast your collection into the local book bank, make sure that you have given them your fullest attention.

Key Source: Books and the Family Bible

For most families before the mid-twentieth century, books would have been something of a luxury. Practical manuals of one sort or another might have been justified on a small household budget, but novels and special-interest books would have been the preserve of the fairly well-off. Most families in the nineteenth century, however, would have had a Bible. If they were wealthy, your family may have possessed a heavy, leather-bound and (by the end of the nineteenth century) richly-illustrated edition. From 1804 onwards, the British and Foreign Bible Society made cheaper editions of the Bible increasingly available to the poor.

In Victorian Britain, the Bible was a prized possession often handed down through many generations. Bibles had a multiple function in the family home, providing spiritual comfort, entertainment (often the family would read from them on Sundays) and education (sometimes a Bible provided the only means by which a child could learn to read). But, most importantly, as far as you might be concerned, Bibles often had another purpose: to act as a repository of information about the history of the family over several generations.

How can I find my family Bible?
If your family Bible isn't lurking in the attic or in a box in the garage, there are a number of different ways you can try to locate it:

- contact as many different branches of your family as possible and ask whether or not they remember the existence of a Bible and if so, what its whereabouts might be
- try the churches, libraries, historical or genealogical societies local to the area in which your family lived
- online. In America, Bible preservation is big business and there are many websites (for example, www.Biblerecords.com) where the information in family Bibles has been scanned and then transcribed so that it is available to all interested parties. The website www.torrens. org.uk/BFB aims to provide the same service for British Family Bibles.
- the auction site Ebay (www.ebay.com) always has a number of family Bibles up for sale.

The Gladwin Family Bible. (With thanks to Mr Tim New)

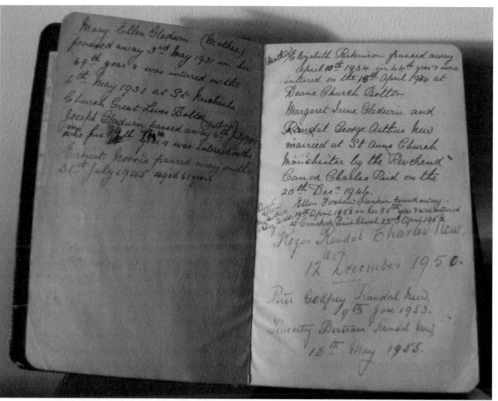

Certain aspects of the family tree are more apparent in entries written in list form than they are in the more modern family tree diagram, for example, the frequency with which certain Christian names were repeated over the generations. (With thanks to Mr Tim New)

What can I find out about my ancestors from a family Bible?
Once you find your family Bible, you need to locate the genealogical information. Usually, this will be written on the inside of the front cover or on its flyleaf. Sometimes a 'Register' (a single page with ruled lines) was printed inside the Bible specifically to allow the recording of family tree information. Occasionally the information is to be found on the blank pages between the Old and New Testaments, but you should also check for handwriting behind loose pictures in the Bible, and in the margins of the text.

There is no doubt that the advantages to a family historian of finding a family Bible can be enormous. It can save weeks of work by providing you with information about many generations and various branches of your family all at once. If the entries were written one by one as the events

171

occurred, then it is likely that they are fairly accurate. Bible records that combine names and dates with places where events took place can significantly help speed up searches for certificates at record offices.

Bible entries may include:

- dates of births, marriages, deaths
- dates of christenings and burials
- the places in which births, marriages and deaths, christenings and burials took place
- causes of death
- dates of when family members enlisted in the army
- the maiden names of women marrying into the family
- records of church membership or membership of other organisations
- the names of godparents
- an indication of which parts of the Bible were read out at births, marriages and deaths.

Think laterally

The condition and type of Bible owned by your family can give you an insight into the kind of people your ancestors were. Your Bible may exhibit signs of heavy use (indicating that the family may have been fairly devout) and certain biblical passages may be marked as special by underscorings in the text. Other Bibles may have marginal notes which indicate which passages were read out at family occasions such as funerals or christenings. Look carefully as well at the types of supplemental material included in your Bible such as maps and commentaries, as these may tell you something about how seriously your family undertook religious study.

Make sure that you check the Bible's date of publication. Sometimes this can be difficult as title pages may be missing or torn. If the title page of the Old Testament is missing, check to see if there is a title page for the New Testament. Then compare the date of publication of the Bible with the date of the first entry made by your ancestor. Was the family tree started when the Bible was bought, or was much of the information written in retrospect? If the latter is the case, the entries (since they would have been made from memory) are less likely to be accurate.

If a lot of entries appear to have been made by the same hand and at the same time, this can indicate that some of the information was transcribed from another source and you need to be aware that mistakes might have been made. Compare the person's handwriting with other examples of family handwriting that you might have to help you decide whether or not the same person did indeed make all the entries. It is also worth asking yourself whether the person who made the entries was actually in attendance at the event recorded – this is particularly important if the event occurred in another country. Entries that have been made out of chronological sequence or squeezed in between others to force them into sequence may also be inaccurate.

Resources to Take You Further
Books
Branston, Barry, *Graphology Explained: A Workbook*, Red Wheel/ Weiser, 1991.

Castle, Egerton, *English Book-Plates: An Illuminated Hand-Book for the Students of Ex-Libris*, Create Space Independent Publishing Platform, 2014.

Jackson, H. J., *Marginalia: Readers Writing in Books*, Yale Nota Bene UP, 2001.

Jackson, H. J., *Romantic Readers: The Evidence of Marginalia,* Yale UP, 2005.

Hopkinson, Martin, *Ex Libris: The Art of the Bookplate,* British Museum Press, 2011.

Lee, Brian North, *British Bookplates: A Pictorial History,* David and Charles, 1979.

Plimpton, George, *The Art of the Bookplate,* Barnes and Noble, 2003.

West, Peter, *The Handwriting Analyst's Tool Kit: Character and Personality Revealed Through Graphology,* Fair Winds Press, 2004.

Websites
www.Biblerecords.com Images and transcripts of genealogical information in Bibles (mainly American).

www.bookplatesociety.org The Bookplate Society – International society of collectors, bibliophiles, artists and others dedicated to promoting bookplate study.

www.miragebookmark.ch/wb_0_directory.htm. Information database on bookmarks.

www.newyorker.com/books/page-turner/the-marginal-obsession-with-marginalia Useful article on marginalia in the *New Yorker*.

www.nls.uk/privatelivesofbooks/ Part of the National Library of Scotland's website showing how inscriptions, signatures, bookplates and bindings can tell us more about the people who owned certain books.

www.torrens.org.uk/BFB/ British Family Bibles. Helps people to locate their family Bible. Provides transcriptions of genealogical information in Bibles that it has acquired.

CHAPTER 12

'You Are What They Ate'

Focus on History: Geography, Culture, Religion and Wealth
Key Source: Recipes, Food and Eating Habits

If you listen carefully to family stories from the past you will be surprised by how many of them revolve around food and drink. You may have heard, for example, how your grandparents used to make a chicken last all week, or how Uncle Brian's side of the family never touched alcohol. Great-grandmother may have used different crockery for meat and milk dishes, or your engine-driver great uncle may have fried bacon on a shovel in his firebox! The stories about food are endless, but none of them should be taken at face value. All of them can tell you something about the social conditions in which your family lived and many other things as well.

The Stories
In my family, there are stories about food that concern most of the characters in this book. In the early twenty-first century, I am pleased to report that we are still eating many dishes that would not have looked out of place on a dining table in Wigan in the 1880s. My mother makes the staple meals of Lancashire 'hash' and Lancashire hotpot with the cuts of beef ('skirt' and 'shin beef') that have traditionally been used in these dishes. There is broth made with brisket, 'meat' stew with barley, roasted cows' hearts and tongue for tea on Sundays. Pickled onions in vinegar are a familiar condiment and my mother enjoys the occasional meal of tripe and onions (though I hasten to add it is not something I have tried!).

So what does this tell me about my family history? It's worth remembering that recipes and eating habits are usually passed down the maternal line. For centuries – probably up until quite recently – women have cooked what their mothers and grandmothers before them cooked with just a few variations according to family size and budget. My mother

'Just like mother used to make': food and eating habits are to some extent inherited and may reveal much about your family origins. (From *The Girl's Own Paper* Vol VII, No. 342. July 1886, in collected volume, *The Girl's Own Annual – Illustrated,* The Leisure Hour Office, 1886, p. 660)

certainly uses recipes that have been passed down to her from her a long line of Wigan women: her mother, grandmother and great-grandmother. What they fed their families tells me something about the economic circumstances of their lives. In short: they had plenty of children and only just enough money to go round: the cuts of meat are the cheapest available; the quantity of meat is small compared with the quantity of potatoes and onions. Vegetables do not appear as a side dish. If they appear at all, they are cooked in the pan with the other ingredients. I am reminded that my Wigan ancestors had probably only a very few basic cooking appliances.

I can analyse further still. There are no fish dishes in our diet – a fact that reminds me that nineteenth-century Wigan was a long way from the sea. In addition, I like to think – perhaps fancifully – that our penchant for pies and pasties at lunchtime harks back to the fact that ancestrally my mother's family worked in mines and factories. This early 'convenience' food would traditionally have been taken from home to the place of work by younger family members. I have also noticed that there aren't many puddings in my mother's culinary repertoire. Perhaps sweets and cakes were a luxury that earlier generations couldn't afford. In fact,

Queuing for meat (1890s): my great-great grandmother probably bought her cheap cuts of lamb and beef at this butcher's shop in Hardybutts, Wigan. (With thanks to Ron Hunt)

the only family story we have about desserts is the rather delightful one about my great-great grandmother, Lydia Fletcher (Chapter 2), who made sweets for her children by dipping the hot poker from her coal fire in sugar until it caramelised!

Food and Health

You may have noticed some odd causes of death on your family certificates. These can attest to a lack of food or food of poor quality in your family household in the past. 'Marasmus' – a wasting of the flesh – was commonly cited in the deaths of young children who were deprived of calories and protein. 'Teething' – an odd but commonly given cause of death – may suggest a contamination of milk or other foodstuffs, and the dreaded 'cholera' was spread by contaminated water and food.

They loved it or loathed it

Sometimes the link between food and family history takes a little bit of untangling. I was always told that my maternal great-grandfather, George Wilkinson (Chapter 8) could 'make a meal out of an orange'. Once I had recognised that there was something a little special about that fact, I started to ask questions of older family members and it was then that I was told that the gentleman in question had apparently insisted on oranges as a treat for his children after he returned from his trip to America in the first decade of the twentieth century. According to family legend, George had been fascinated by the sheer proliferation of the citrus fruits at the American table. Over there, he had oranges in salads, orange milk sherbert, orange sauce, and orange jelly. Back in Wigan, the oranges were just oranges – but, nevertheless, they were greeted with glee by my grandfather's children, particularly when George made them boats out of the orange peel to sail down the local gutters when they filled with rain.

Family history can be revealed as much through the foodstuffs and beverages that your family will not eat and drink as much as through those that they love. My father (William Symes, Chapter 5) maintained a lifelong loathing of Vimto and corned beef because they reminded him of the Second World War years. My great-aunts Emmie, Phyllis and Jenny Symes (Chapter 7) whom I knew when I was a young child and when they were very old ladies, never touched a drop of alcohol. Having investigated their mother's death (Elizabeth Symes in Chapter 6) and discovered evidence of her strict Methodism, I now understand that this abstinence was a matter of religious principle as much as a personal preference on that side of the family.

The Fruits of Marriage

Marriages in families bring culinary traditions together. So alongside my mother's Lancashire fare, we had my father's favourites – applesauce and gooseberries. It has recently struck me that these fruity dishes are traditionally South Western delicacies rather than Mancunian fare and I have sometimes wondered whether our enjoyment of such fruit is inherited from my great-grandfather, William Symes who came from the apple orchards and fruit fields of Somerset to Manchester in the late nineteenth century (Chapter 1).

Food also differentiates one culture from another. If your family came to Britain from another country, you will probably find that they brought with them some of their dining habits – including ideas about which foods were special and which taboo. My husband's family have a wonderful cuisine that combines the spices of India with the corn, coconut and yams commonly eaten in Africa. Having traced their ancestry (Chapter 9) back to Tanzania and before that to the North Indian state of Gujarat, I can see how the two cuisines have come together. Friends of mine whose ancestors were Lithuanian Jews, still eat the chopped liver favoured by their ancestors. Pork is, of course, entirely absent from their dining table.

Food from East Africa is still enjoyed on special occasions by the family today. (Author's collection)

Christmas

Christmastime can be an excellent starting point for family history research. Unlike your hastily-compiled weekday menus, habits of eating and drinking at Christmas follow well-established routines redolent of Christmases past. What you traditionally eat and drink at Christmas are matters that have very often been passed down through the family with little change over many generations.

Every Christmas morning we have a drink made from hot cider, eggs and spices. It has a strange but warming taste. I have always been somewhat puzzled by this beverage. Cider, as far as I know, is not a staple of Greater Manchester and Merseyside. So why do we hardened North-Westerners choose to drink it? Some years ago, whilst flicking through a cookery book, I came across a recipe for 'Egg Hot' as it is known. I was delighted to discover that it originated in Devonshire and Somersetshire. There is little doubt about it – this drink must have been passed down to my family by our ancestors from the South West.

Other drinks that are traditionally used to toast Christmas and New Year tell their own tales. Mead, made from honey, lemons, cloves and ginger, may be inherited from Welsh forebears, whilst a range of different

This late nineteenth-century table is laid out to demonstrate how one might entertain a family at supper in a household where the yearly income was £250. It includes pastry, sandwiches, fruit jelly, salad, eggs à la russe, nougats, sweetmeats, galantine of veal, oyster patties, fruit trifle, fancy cakes, gateau napolitain, mocha jelly, apricot cream and fancy pastry. ('How We Entertain Our Friends: The Supper Table', *The Girl's Own Paper* Vol VI. No. 281, 16 May 1885)

recipes for hot toddies could denote ancestors from all sorts of different places including the Shetland Isles (where a festive drink known as 'whipcoll' was made from brandy beaten with eggs, sugar and cream).

You should consider what you eat at Christmas carefully. Most people nowadays eat turkey on Christmas Day – so this, in itself, will tell you little about the history of a particular family – but it is worth thinking a little about your other choices of meat and game during the festive season. If you usually have beef, it is possible that this is a legacy of ancestors from the North of England, people with southern ancestors may gravitate towards goose, and those with an Irish heritage towards pork. Eating fish on Christmas Eve may indicate a Catholic or an Italian heritage, whilst a meal of rabbit may hark back to a time when your family was too poor to feast on other sorts of meat.

An Irish cook working in an English household in the mid-nineteenth century. Food traditions have been brought to Britain by all our immigrant ancestors.
(Illustration to story, 'Love Light: Being the Christmas Number of the *Girl's Own Paper'*, 1891, in *The Girl's Own Annual,* The Leisure Hour Office, 1891, p. 13)

Every county in Britain has had its unique ways of making seasonal pies and puddings – look out for these. A time-honoured tradition of making a Cumberland Sweet Pie or Yorkshire Christmas Pie for Boxing Day will probably be explicable in terms of your family history, and even the widely-eaten Yule Log (or *Buche de Noel*) could be a clue to French ancestry. Look out too for puddings made without eggs – they could be a legacy from the rationing of the Second World War.

Potentially the most interesting Christmas dish of all from a family history point of view is the pudding. If you make yours from an old family recipe, think carefully about what the ingredients may tell you about the life of your ancestors. Very religious families may have made the pudding with a traditional range of thirteen ingredients (representing Christ and his twelve disciples). In my family, the pudding is made without brandy indicating the family history of temperance. Many working-class socialists in the late nineteenth and early twentieth centuries would have shunned the addition of alcohol. Some middle-class versions of the Christmas pudding on the other hand were liberally laced with rum. You might also think a little about the non-edible items traditionally placed inside the pudding. Poor families may have stirred sixpences into the recipe, but richer families would traditionally have added silver trinkets.

Of course, not just *what* you eat and drink but *when* and *how* you eat and drink it may be of relevance to your search for clues about your history. The tradition in some families of eating the main meal on Christmas Eve may indicate that your ancestors originated in another European country such as Germany where festivities traditionally start a day early. Fasting on Christmas Eve, on the other hand, may be something inherited from Polish ancestors. And what about the length of your festivities? Italian-inspired Christmas celebrations may last several weeks whereas Protestant British ones may be over in a couple of days.

Etiquette

Food is integral to the management and manners of a household. If your family tends to eat certain foods on certain days of the week, you should consider when and where this habit originated. Behaviour around food such as the times of dining, the etiquette for asking to be excused, and the way a table is laid (or cleared), may all have been inherited from earlier generations.

Christmas is useful from a family history point of view because it is, of course, the period when all the different generations (and perhaps also some of the branches) of the family are in one place and with plenty of time on their hands. What better opportunity could there be to stir up old memories? Festive food and drink and the customs around them naturally give rise to questions about the past from younger family members and, with luck, you may glean some helpful answers from older generations. Indeed this is perhaps the most important aspect of stories about food in family history – they provide a means of getting the younger generation interested in their origins. Where censuses and death certificates may leave them uninspired, a spicy carrot cake or something similar may well just do the trick!

Key Source: Recipes, Food and Eating Habits

Even when other 'more important' sources of genealogical information, such as wills, family bibles, and birth and death certificates, are lost, family recipes and even family habits of eating are often passed down intact from generation to generation.

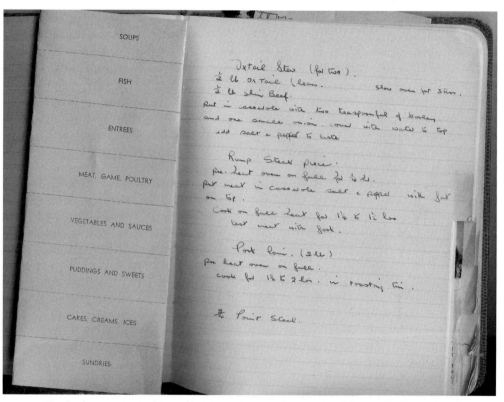

Handwritten recipe books passed down from mothers to daughters on their marriage may include the annotations of many generations. (With thanks to Olive Symes)

How can I find out more about my family's eating habits?

Family cookery books can give a useful insight into various aspects of your family's daily life in the past. If you have one, you can assume that whoever first used it had a certain level of literacy. If it is a published cookery book such as Mrs Beeton's famous *Book of Household Management* (first edition, 1861), be careful not to make too many

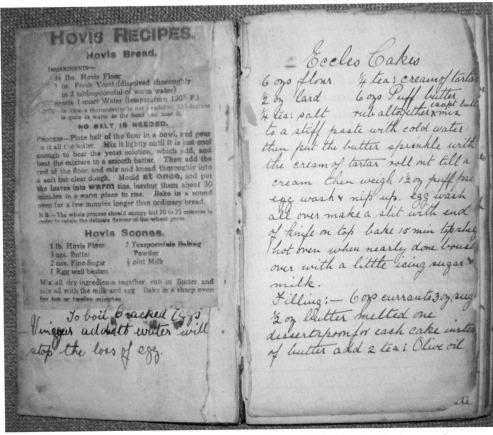

This cookery book which was used between 1920 and 1940 has handwritten entries and recipes pasted in from newspapers. One here for Eccles Cakes betrays the author's roots in the North West. (With thanks to Tim New)

assumptions from it about the way your family ate in the past. Such books probably tell you more about how your ancestors *aspired* to eat than what they actually ate.

Handwritten recipes are probably a more accurate record of what actually appeared on your ancestors' plates. If you do come across such a book, it is worth having a go at sourcing the ingredients and making some of the dishes. There is nothing quite like the excitement of taking your first mouthful of food from a recipe once cooked by your great-

184

grandmother – to taste the tastes that once satisfied the earlier generations of your family. Be careful, however, you may want to substitute some of the more old-fashioned ingredients such as 'rendered goose fat' for modern equivalents such as butter or oil!

What can I learn about my ancestors from family recipes and stories about food?
You may learn something about the following:

• the individual preferences of certain family members
• your ancestors' country and region of origin
• their culture
• their religious beliefs
• their attitude to alcohol
• their income level and class status
• the size and composition of their families.

Think laterally
Listen carefully to the language that is used by older members of your family to describe certain dishes – unusual words and phrases such as 'moggies', 'lobscouse' and 'chilli chicken' may alert you to the fact that your ancestors came from – or had experiences in – other places such as Yorkshire, Liverpool or India.

It is worth thinking about the way in which your family has traditionally made foods such as bread and cakes, or how they have prepared stews and puddings. The ingredients and techniques used may tell you something about what foodstuffs were available in their locality in the past – their proximity to the sea, their access to fresh (as opposed to preserved) food, for example.

Of course, you must be careful not to read too much into family stories about food. In recent years, we have all become much more wide-ranging in our food tastes as food from all over the country and all over the world has become available to us at relatively cheap prices. Nevertheless, there is still, I think, something to be learned from particular family anecdotes, and it is certainly important to continue the traditions.

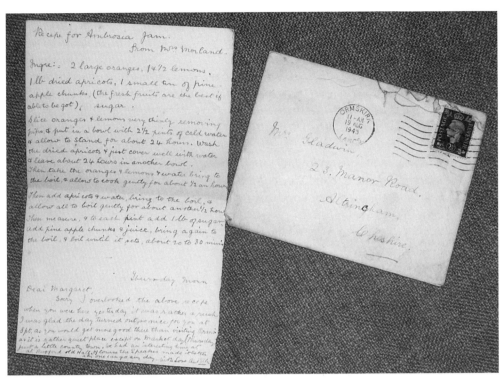

Between women: this letter written in 1949 from Ellen Hankin to her niece, Margaret Alice Gladwin, includes a recipe for Ambrosia Jam. (With thanks to Tim New)

Resources to Take You Further

Books

Burnett, John, *Plenty and Want: A Social History of Diet in England from 1815 to the Present Day*, 3rd edition, Routledge, 1989.

Gwynn, Mary, *Back in Time for Dinner: From Spam to Sushi: How We've Changed the Way We Eat*, Bantam Press, 2015.

Hughes, Kathryn, *The Short Life and Long Times of Mrs Beeton*, Fourth Estate, 2005.

Mabey, David, *Traditional Eating and Drinking in Britain, A Feast of Regional Foods*, Macdonald and James, 1978.

McGee, Harold, *McGee on Food and Cooking: An Encyclopedia of Kitchen Science, History and Culture*, Hodder and Stoughton, 2004.

King, Si and Myers, Dave, *The Hairy Bikers' Food Tour of Britain*, Weidenfeld and Nicolson, 2009.

Richardson, Paul, *Cornucopia: A Gastronomic Tour of Britain*, Abacus, 2002.

Tannahill, Reay, *Food in History*, Eyre Methuen, 1973.

Wright, Clarissa Dickson, *A History of English Food*, Random House, 2011.

Websites

www.bbc.co.uk/history/topics/rationing_in_ww2 BBC History site on rationing in the Second World War.

www.foodmuseum.com Food history, news, features and temporary exhibits.

www.foodsofengland.co.uk/ Holds the complete text of dozens of old cookbooks.

www.foodtimeline.org Timeline of American and world food history.

www.historic-uk.com/CultureUK/History-of-British-Food/ The History and Heritage Accommodation Guide with a brief history of British food.

www.oxfordsymposium.org.uk/blog/ Blog for the Oxford Symposium on Food and Cookery. This brings together writers, historians, sociologists, anthropologists, scientists, chefs and others who specialise in the study of food in history, its place in contemporary societies and related scientific developments. It also lists museums throughout the world dedicated to food.

www.visitbritain.com/en/Things-to-do/Food/Unique-British-foods.html Visit Britain's guide to unique British foods.

Addresses

York Castle Museum

Eye of York

Y01 9RY

Bibliography

Adburgham, Alison, *Shops and Shopping, 1800-1914*, Allen and Unwin, 1964.

Anuta, Michael J., *Ships of our Ancestors*, Menominee. 1983.

Arnot, Chris, *Britain's Lost Mines: The Vanished Kingdom of the Men Who Carved Out the Nation's Wealth*, Aurum Press, 2013.

Aughton, Peter, *Liverpool: A People's History*, Carnegie Publishing, 1990.

Ayers, Pat, *Liverpool Docklands*, Liver Press, 1999.

Baranick, Alana, Sheeler, Jim, and Miller, Stephen, *Life on the Death Beat: A Handbook for Obituary Writers*, Marion Street Press, 2005.

Baren, Maurice E., *Victorian Shopping: How it All Began*, Michael O'Mara, 1998.

Barratt, Nick, *Who Do You Think You Are? Encyclopedia of Genealogy: The Definitive Reference Guide to Tracing Your Family Tree*, Harper, 2008.

Batts, John Stuart, *British Manuscript Diaries of the Nineteenth Century: An Annotated Listing*, Rowman and Littlefield, 1976.

Bevan, Judi, *The Rise and Fall of Marks and Spencer*, Profile Books. 2001.

Bookbinder, Paul, *Marks and Spencer: The War Years, 1939-1945*, Century Benham, 1989.

Branston, Barry, *Graphology Explained: A Workbook*, Red Wheel/Weiser, 1991.

Briggs, Asa, *Marks and Spencer: 1884-1984: A Centenary History of Marks and Spencer: The Originators of Penny Bazaars*, Octopus Books, 1984.

Broad, Richard, and Fleming, Suzie (eds), *Nella Last's War: The Second World War Diaries of Housewife 49*, Profile Books, 2006.

Brockington, Colin Fraser, *A Short History of Public Health*, Churchill, 1956.

Brooks, C., *Mortal Remains: The History and Present State of the Victorian Cemetery*, Wheaton, 1989.

Brunskill, Ian (ed.), *Great Lives: A Century in Obituaries*, Times Books, 2006.

Burnett, John, *Plenty and Want: A Social History of Diet in England from 1815 to the Present Day*, 3rd edition, Routledge, 1989.

Butterworth, Annie, *Manual of Household Work and Management*, Longmans, Green, and Co., 1913.

Castle, Egerton, *English Book-Plates: An Illuminated Hand-Book for the Students of Ex-Libris*, Create Space Independent Publishing Platform, 2014.

Catlett, Estelle, *Track Down Your Ancestors: Draw Up Your Family Tree*, Elliot Right Way Books, 2003.

Chapman, Colin R., *An Introduction to Using Newspapers and Periodicals*, Federation of Family History Societies, 1993.

Chater, Kathy, *How to Trace Your Family Tree in England, Ireland, Scotland and Wales*, Hermes House/Anness Publishing, 2006.

Chislett, Helen, *Marks in Time: 125 Years of Marks and Spencer*, W & N, 2009.

Clarke, Eric, *The Story of Sainsbury's*, Hutchinson, 1999.

BIBLIOGRAPHY

Cole, Jean A., Armstrong, Michael, and Titford, John, *Tracing Your Family Tree: The Comprehensive Guide to Tracing Your Family History (Genealogy)* , Countryside Books, 2003.

Coleman, Terry, *A History of Emigrants from Great Britain and Ireland to America in the Mid-Nineteenth Century*, Pimlico, 1992.

Colletta, John P., *They Came in Ships: A Guide to Finding Your Immigrant Ancestor's Arrival Record*, Ancestry rpt, 1993.

Creaton, Heather, *Victorian Diaries: The Daily Lives of Victorian Men and Women*, Mitchell Beazely, 2001.

Cullwick, Hannah, *The Diaries of Hannah Cullwick. Victorian Maidservant*, Rutgers UP, 1984.

Davidoff, Leonore, 'The Separation of Home and Work? Landladies and Lodgers in Nineteenth- and Twentieth-Century England', in Burman, Sandra, *Fit Work for Women*, Croom Helm, 1979.

Davis, Dorothy, *A History of Shopping*, Routledge, 2010.

Davis, Gayle, *'The Cruel Madness of Love': Sex, Syphilis and Psychiatry in Scotland, 1880-1930*, Rodopi, 2008.

Galford, Ellen and Ancestry.com, *The Genealogy Handbook: The Complete Guide to Tracing Your Family Tree*, Reader's Digest Association, 2005.

Filby, William P., *Passenger and Immigration Lists Bibliography 1538-1900: Being a Guide to Published Lists of Arrivals in the United States and Canada*, 2nd edition, Gale Research Co, 1988.

Garfield, Simon, *We Are At War: The Remarkable Diaries of Five Ordinary People in Extraordinary Times*, Ebury Press, 2006.

Ghai, Dharam P., *Portrait of a Minority: Asians in East Africa*, Oxford UP, 1965.

Gibson, J. S. W., *Local Census Listings*, Federation of Family History Societies, 1992.

Gibson, J., Langston B., and Smith, B. W., *Local Newspapers, 1750-1920: England and Wales, Channel Islands, and the Isle of Man, a Select Location List*, 2nd edition, Federation of Family History Societies, 2002.

Gill, Anton and Barratt, Nick, *Who Do You Think You Are? Trace Your Family History Back to the Tudors*, HarperCollins Entertainment, 2006.

Girl's Own Paper, The, Vol VII, No. 342. July 1886, in *The Illustrated Girl's Own Annual*, The Leisure Hour Office, 1886.

Gwynn, Mary, *Back in Time for Dinner: From Spam to Sushi: How We've Changed the Way We Eat*, Bantam Press, 2015.

Hadfield. Charles, *British Canals: An Illustrated History*, David and Charles, 1974.

Herber, Mark, *Ancestral Trails: The Complete Guide to British Genealogy and Family History*, 2nd edition, Sutton Publishing, 1997.

Heritage, Celia, *Tracing Your Ancestors Through Death Records: A Guide For Family Historians*, Pen and Sword Books, 2013.

Higgs, E., *A Clearer Sense of the Census: The Victorian Censuses and Historical Research*, HMSO, 1996.

Higgs, E., *Making Sense of the Census; The Manuscript Returns for England and Wales, 1801-1901*, HMSO, 1989.

Higgs, Michelle, *Tracing Your Servant Ancestors*, Pen and Sword, 2012

Hindle, B. P., *Maps for Local History*, Batsford, 1988.

Hoffman, P.C., *They Also Serve: The Story of the Shopworker*, Porcupine Press, 1949.

Hollingsworth, Lawrence William, *The Asians of East Africa*, Macmillan, 1960.

Hopkinson, Martin, *Ex Libris: The Art of the Bookplate*, British Museum Press, 2011.

Horn, Pamela, *The Rise and Fall of the Domestic Servant*, Alan Sutton, 1986.

Hoskins, W. G., *Local History in England*, 3rd edition, Longman, 1984.

Hughes, Kathryn, *The Short Life and Long Times of Mrs Beeton*, Fourth Estate, 2005.

Jackson, H. J., *Marginalia: Readers Writing in Books*, Yale Nota Bene UP, 2001.

Jackson, H. J., *Romantic Readers: The Evidence of Marginalia*, Yale UP, 2005.

Jalland, Pat, *Death in the Victorian Family*, OUP, 1996.

Kennedy, Carol, *Business Pioneers: Sainsbury, John Lewis, Cadbury*, Random House Business Books, 2001.

Kershaw, R., *Emigrants and Ex Pats: A Guide to Sources on UK Emigration and Residents Overseas*, PRO, 2000.

Kershaw, R. and Pearsall, M., *Immigrants and Aliens: A Guide to Sources on UK Immigration and Citizenship*, PRO, 2000.

King, Si, and Myers, Dave, *The Hairy Bikers' Food Tour of Britain*, Weidenfeld and Nicolson, 2009.

Kraut, Alan M., *The Huddled Masses: The Immigrant in American Society, 1880-1921*, Harlan Davidson, 2001.

Lee, Brian North, *British Bookplates: A Pictorial History*, David and Charles, 1979.

Lethbridge, Lucy, *Servants: A Downstairs View of Twentieth-Century Britain*, Bloomsbury, 2013.

Litten, Julian, *The English Way of Death*, Robert Hale, 2002.

Lloyd, Martin, *The Passport: The History of Man's Most Travelled Document*, Sutton Publishing, 2003.

Lobo, Lois, *They Came to Africa: Two Hundred Years of the Asian Presence in Tanzania*, Sustainable Village, 2000.

'Love Light: Being the Christmas Number of the *Girl's Own Paper*' in *The Girl's Own Annual*, The Leisure Hour Office, 1891.

Lumas, S., *Making Use of the Census*, 4th edition, PRO, 2002.

Maber, Roy, *Martock Memories: A Hundred Years of Village Life*, Norman Maber and Associates, 1975.

Maber, Roy, *More Martock Memories: The Story of a Somerset Village*, Matthew Maber, 1993.

Mabey, David, *Traditional Eating and Drinking in Britain: A Feast of Regional Foods*, Macdonald and James, 1978.

Maloney, Alison, *Life Below Stairs: True Lives of Edwardian Servants*, Michael O'Mara, 2011.

Marchant, Brian, *Boots the Chemist of Nottingham on Old Picture Postcards: Yesterday's Nottinghamshire*, Reflections of a Byegone Age, 1999.

BIBLIOGRAPHY

Mangat, J. S., *A History of Asians in East Africa c. 1886-1945*, Clarendon, 1969.

Matthews, William, *British Diaries: An Annotated Bibliography of British Diaries Written Between 1442 and 1942*, California UP, 1992.

Maw, Peter, *Transport and the Industrial City: Manchester and the Canal Age, 1750-1850*, Manchester University Press, 2013.

Maxted, Ian, *British National Directories 1781-1819: an Index to Places in the British Isles Included in Trade Directories with General Provincial Coverage*, Exeter Working Papers in British Book Trade History, 1989.

May, Trevor, *The Victorian Domestic Servant*, Shire, 1999.

May, Trevor, *Victorian Undertaker*, Shire, 1996.

Mbogani, Lawrence E. Y., *Aspects of Colonial Tanzania History*, Mkuki Na Nyota Publishers, 2013.

McGee, Harold, *McGee on Food and Cooking: An Encyclopedia of Kitchen Science, History and Culture*, Hodder and Stoughton, 2004.

McGregor, Alexandrina, *A Chapbook of Memories of Marks and Spencer: From 1946 to 1980*, East Wittering, 1994.

McHugh, Paul, *Prostitution and Victorian Social Reform*, Croom Helm, 1980.

McLaughlin, E., *Family History from Newspapers*, Family Tree Magazine, 1994.

McLaughlin, E., *Illegitimacy*, 5th edition, Federation of Family History Societies, 1992.

Melling, Dhyll, *Historic Trade Directories in Guildhall Library*, Guildhall Library Publications, 2005.

Mills, Dennis R., *Rural Community History from Trade Directories*, Aldenham, Local Population Studies, 2001.

Norton, J. E., *Guide to the National and Provincial Directories of England and Wales (excluding London) published before 1856*, Royal Historical Society, 1950.

Novotny, Ann, *Strangers at the Door*, The Chatham Press, 1971.

Osborn, Helen, *Genealogy: Essential Research Methods*, Robert Hale Ltd, 2012.

Pandit, Shanti, *Asians in East and Central Africa*, Nairobi, 1961.

Paquet, Laura, *The Urge to Splurge: A Social History of Shopping*, E.C.W. Press, 2004.

Plimpton, George, *The Art of the Bookplate*, Barnes and Noble, 2003.

Porter, Roy (ed.), *The Illustrated Cambridge History of Medicine*, CUP, 2001.

Porter, Roy, and Hall, Lesley, *The Facts of Life: The Creation of Sexual Knowledge in Britain 1650-1950*, Yale UP, 1995.

Quetel, Claude, *History of Syphilis*, Polity Press, 1992.

Richardson, Paul, *Cornucopia: A Gastronomic Tour of Britain*, Abacus, 2002.

Roberts, Elizabeth, *A Woman's Place: An Oral History of Working-Class Women, 1890-1940*, Blackwell, 1986.

Rogers, Colin, *The Family Tree Detective: Tracing Your Ancestors in England and Wales*, Manchester UP, 1997.

Rogers, C., and Smith, J. H., *Local Family History in England. 1538-1914*, M.U.P., 1991.

Seidenberg, Dana April, *Mercantile Adventurers: The World Of East African Asians, 1750-1985*, New Age International Publishers, 1986.

191

Shaw, G., and Tipper, A., *British Directories: A Bibliography and Guide to Directories Published in England and Wales (1880-1950); & Scotland (1773-1950)* , 2nd edition, Leicester UP, 1997.

Shaw, William Arthur, *Manchester Old and New with Illustrations after Original Drawings by H. E. Tidmarsh*, Vols 1–3, Cassell and Co., 1896.

Sheridan, Dorothy, *Wartime Women: A Mass-Observation Anthology of Women's Writings 1937-1945*, W & N, 2009.

Shideler, John C., *Coal Towns in the Cascades: A Centennial History of Roslyn and Cle Elum, Washington*, Melior Publications, 1986.

Starck, Nigel, *Life after Death: A Celebration of the Obituary Art*, Melbourne UP, 2006.

Steele, Jess, *Rations and Rubble – Remembering Woolworths*, Deptford Forum Publishing, 1994.

Tannahill, Reay, *Food in History*, Eyre Methuen, 1973.

Times, The, *Tercentenary Handlist of English and Welsh Newspapers, Magazines and Reviews, 1620-1919* (Times Publishing Co., 1920), Dawson reprint, 1966.

Tonks, David, *My Ancestor was a Coalminer*, Society of Genealogists' Enterprises Ltd, 2003.

Torpey, John, *The Invention of the Passport: Surveillance, Citizenship and the State*, Cambridge UP, 2000.

Visram, Rosina, *Asians in Britain: 400 Years of History*, Pluto Press, 2002.

Waddell, Dan, *Who Do You Think You Are? The Genealogy Handbook*, BBC Books, 2014.

Walton, John, *The Blackpool Landlady*, Manchester UP, 1978.

Ward, Margaret, *The Female Line: Researching Your Female Ancestors*, Countryside Books, 2003.

West, Peter, *The Handwriting Analyst's Tool Kit: Character and Personality Revealed Through Graphology*, Fair Winds Press, 2004.

Whitaker, Wilfred, *Victorian and Edwardian Shopworkers: The Struggle to Obtain Better Working Conditions and a half Holiday*, David and Charles, 1973.

Whittington-Egan, Richard, *The Great Liverpool Blitz*, The Gallery Press, 1987.

Wigan Directory, J. Worral, 1869 (rpt. Neil Richardson, 1983).

Wittke, Carl F., *We Who Built America: The Saga of the Immigrant*, Western Reserve UP, 1964.

Wright, Clarissa Dickson, *A History of English Food*, Random House, 2011.

Wright, G., *Discovering Epitaphs*, Shire, 2003.

Index

Page numbers in *italics* refer to illustrations.

193